GROW
SMART,

A Low-Capital Path *to* Multiplying
Your Business Through Franchising

RISK
LESS

SHELLY SUN

GREENLEAF
BOOK GROUP PRESS

Disclaimer of warranty:

The publisher and the author make no representations or warranties with respect to the accuracy or completeness of the contents of this work, and all of the contents are provided on an "as is" basis. To the fullest extent permitted by law, the publisher and the author specifically disclaim all warranties, whether express, implied, arising by statute, custom, course of dealing, course of performance or in any other way, with respect to this work. Without limiting the generality of the foregoing, the publisher and the author disclaim all representations and warranties (a) of title, non-infringement, merchantability and fitness for a particular purpose or (b) that the contents of this work are accurate, complete or current. No warranty may be created or extended by sales or promotional materials.

The advice and strategies contained herein may not be suitable for every company or every situation. Objectives, strategies, practices, decisions and results will vary depending on many factors. This work is sold with the understanding that neither the publisher nor author is engaged in rendering legal, accounting, or other professional services. If professional assistance is required, the services of a competent professional should be sought. The fact that an organization or website is referred to in this work as a citation and/or a potential source of further information does not mean that the author or the publisher endorses the information the organization or website may provide or recommendations it may make. Further, readers should be aware that Internet websites listed in this work may have changed or disappeared between when this work was written and when it is read.

Limitation of liability:

To the fullest extent permitted by applicable laws, the publisher and author exclude and disclaim liability for any losses and expenses of whatever nature and howsoever arising including, without limitation, any direct, indirect, general, special, punitive, incidental or consequential damages; loss of income or profit; loss of or damage to property; claims of third parties; or other losses of any kind or character, even if we have been advised of the possibility of such damages or losses, arising out of or in connection with this work. This limitation of liability applies whether the alleged liability is based on contract, tort (including negligence), strict liability or any other basis.

If any part of this limitation on liability is found to be invalid or unenforceable for any reason, then the aggregate liability of the released parties for liabilities that otherwise would have been limited shall not exceed ten dollars ($10.00).

Part of the Tree Neutral® program, which offsets the number of trees consumed in the production and printing of this book by taking proactive steps, such as planting trees in direct proportion to the number of trees used: www.treeneutral.com

TreeNeutral

Printed in the United States of America on acid-free paper

11 12 13 14 15 16 10 9 8 7 6 5 4 3 2 1

First Edition

Contents

Preface

I have often wondered why people write books. What motivated them, and how long did they plan to do it? Is it fulfilling a lifelong dream? I didn't plan to write a book and didn't know I was going to do so. But I benefited so much from great mentoring in my first five years in franchising, and I so enjoy being able to share ideas and best practices, that Brian Schnell, my dear friend, mentor, and attorney, recommended that I consider starting a consulting company to help franchisors "do it right." That turned out to be the first step toward my writing *Grow Smart, Risk Less*.

With the thought of a consulting company still percolating in my mind, I headed out a few weeks later to deliver the keynote speech at Nova Southeastern University's Emerging Franchisor Conference. Afterward, several attendees came up and said, "You should write a book. Take these lessons and expand them into full chapters." With running a company and being a wife and the mother of twin five-year-old boys, I wondered if I would ever find the time to seriously consider the suggestions. About a month later, however, I found myself thinking about this idea once again, and that proved to be the second step toward my commitment to write this book. Our success has not been our own but rather the result of active involvement with the International Franchise Association (IFA) and the people I met in franchising who so openly shared their good and sometimes not-so-good experiences. Thinking of how much help I received from others during our successful franchise journey helped me decide to write a book to help other potential franchisors start strong and, most important, continue with business practices that will enable them to stay strong and start more businesses that create more jobs and spur much-needed economic growth during challenging economic times. At the end of the day, my goal is to help franchisors improve so their franchisees have greater support that enables long-term success. Without question, enabling business ownership for franchisees and focusing on their success is what characterizes the most successful franchisors.

The journey of BrightStar (referred to as "BrightStar" throughout to speak of the enterprise; if a position or program is exclusively for the BrightStar Care brand, then BrightStar Care will be used) began with our first company-owned location in 2002. My husband and I founded our company because we were passionate about delivering high-quality home care to those in need after having our own challenging experience with home care. We didn't know how we would scale to serve families everywhere, but that was our desire from the beginning, which we included in our original business plan. To scale and offer consistent service and quality required us to have world-class technology, so we invested in proprietary software early. With technology and talented personnel in place, we began thinking about expansion. One of our main concerns was whether we would be able to keep our unique BrightStar culture if we raised money through private equity to open our own locations everywhere. We also wondered whether we could find employees in *all* locations to treat the customers as we wanted them to be treated.

Ask and you shall receive. Divine intervention forever changed our path as we took an opportunity in July 2004 to invest in two hotels and thus became franchisees of two different franchise systems. I attended new owner and manager training classes. I read the operations manuals cover to cover; I am most likely in a minority of franchisees in history to do so. I saw what I loved about being a franchisee and what I would change if I had a magic wand. I began to fashion my own magic wand and decided in October 2004 to apply it to franchising our business model.

As sometimes happens in life, we were thrown a curveball. We were pregnant with twin boys, and about five months into our pregnancy I went on doctor-ordered bed rest. Knowing my chronic workaholic tendencies, my dear husband, J.D., helped save my sanity by having a swivel table delivered so I could put a computer on it and work while in bed. My staff indulged me with weekly staff meetings in my bedroom. What do you do when you have a big block of time and you want to launch a franchise company? You write the operations manuals, and that is exactly what I did over the next five weeks. I filed our legal entity from bed on January 21, 2005. One week later, our boys were born at twenty-eight weeks: Luc weighing in at two pounds, fifteen ounces, and Mike at three pounds, one ounce. We now had beautiful twin boys in the NICU (Luc stayed there fifteen weeks and Mike thirteen), a newly formed franchise company, and two company-owned locations. I craved routine and needed to maintain some semblance of control, so I began getting up at 4:00 a.m., heading to the office where I would work until about 2:00 p.m., and then driving over to the hospital with J.D. and staying with our sons until about 10:00 or 11:00 p.m. I still work a lot because I love what I do. Occasionally an employee or franchisee will receive an e-mail at two o'clock in the morning and reply with a comment wondering how I can work so late into the night. The hours I keep now pale in comparison to those days before we brought the boys home.

With the boys at home in April 2005, we began preparing the legal documents (called an offering circular or franchise disclosure document) to offer our franchise for sale. We filed the offering circular in August. We sold our first franchise in December of that year and opened our first franchise location in March 2006. Five short years later, we have more than 175 franchisees and 250 locations and have invested heavily in technology and a "best in class" team to ensure continued growth and long-term success. We have prepared our organization to leverage our investments to expand domestically, internationally, and into additional brands (across multiple business segments). We continue to set aggressive goals by knowing how our competitors perform in each of the industries in which we will operate, and we then use that information to build our plans to meet and then surpass the segment leaders.

I have a CPA background, so I emphasize measuring and benchmarking and watching trends, areas that are frequently overlooked by many franchisors. For me, being a nerd is second nature, and I have had to spend a great deal of time learning sales processes, skills, and best practices. Most of us are strong in one area and have a second strength in another of the three legs of the stool—sales, operations, and finance. Through this book you will see my first strength is finance and my second is operations, which I hope will benefit those of you with different strengths, just as I have benefited over the years from the sales geniuses in franchising: Rob Goggins, Kurt Landwehr, and Joe Mathews.

In addition to helping you increase your skills and opportunities for ultimate success, I want you to learn from my biggest mistakes. Of course I am not proud of the mistakes, but in my frugal CPA way, I feel that sharing them enhances the opportunity to help others avoid the pitfalls I endured. Therefore, throughout the book I have indicated what I would do again (Bright Idea) and what I would change (Avoid This Pitfall), especially as we launch new brands. To weave in the core strengths that have led to our success—which include benchmarking at the franchisor and franchisee level, ensuring short decision cycles, and investing in technology to grow and scale effectively and efficiently—I have also discussed the key principles of our organization on improving franchisee unit economics, offering a breadth of revenue opportunities, providing high quality and quantity of support, and ensuring strong customer value essential to building and sustaining a strong global brand.

Our focus on culture and systems and learning the best practices of franchising have been the biggest contributors to our success, both financially and in the relationships we have built within the franchise industry, with our franchisees, and with our corporate team. Franchisors can be successful for short periods of time regardless of how their franchisees perform, but the franchisors who enjoy the greatest long-term success follow a model in which the majority of their franchisees can make money, can succeed, and are highly satisfied with the franchisor–franchisee relationship. In particular, the founder/CEO must have passion and commitment to a relentless pursuit of improving franchisee unit economics. This is not something that can be delegated, because the organization will take its direction from how committed the leader is to enabling franchisees' success, to supporting franchisees, and to finding the win-win in the decisions that are made daily.

My goal is to help those of you who are interested in expanding your business through franchising or who are already in franchising—regardless of your role, your years in franchising, or the number of units your franchise system has. If you take away at least one particular idea to implement that will provide a positive return on investment (ROI) for your time in reading this book, then my reasons for writing this book will have been validated.

Much of the content will provide examples from my firsthand experience in the service industry, specifically in healthcare, but I have also tried to call out where differences will exist for concepts in the retail, hospitality, and food industries. While there are industry-specific nuances, particularly with real estate considerations, the steps, the sequence, and the biggest factors in success—the team, the culture, the franchisee–franchisor relationship, the focus on the end customer and technology—are common among all franchise concepts.

Introduction

Have you created a successful business and are now wondering what your options are to expand your business? You have most likely invested a minimum of hundreds of thousands of dollars to build your business, secure trademarks, develop your brand and online presence, document processes, implement technology, and hire staff. You have a solid foundation. Now what?

Opening additional locations on your own could take hundreds of thousands—if not millions—of dollars that are not easy to access through traditional financing today. As you think of ways to leverage the large investments you have made already, consider that franchising can be a great way to scale your brand to more markets, building upon those investments and years of fine-tuning that made your business a success locally. Franchising links your expertise and investments as the franchisor with the capital and personal oversight of a franchisee to replicate your model in a new geographical market. You are able to leverage the passion, commitment, and capital of franchisees to deliver your goods and services to more customers across a larger geographic region. You may want to expand regionally, nationally, or globally, and franchising is the least capital-intensive (and most proven if done right) way to do so, with less risk and more upside potential than any other method of brand expansion.

Launching a franchise brand still requires an additional financial commitment of several hundred thousand dollars by the franchisor to lay and build the franchise system foundation. But to open more company-owned locations requires significantly more capital than opening locations through franchising. Given that lenders are facing a stricter regulatory environment, record high and long-lasting unemployment rates, and less business collateral, creativity and innovative ideas are required to figure out the best way to expand with limited access to capital. The beauty of franchising is that the geographical expansion into new markets also uses the capital of the franchisees, in essence allowing the brand to expand utilizing other people's money.

Franchising spreads the risk between the franchisor and the franchisee. The franchisor has invested in the pilot locations and secured their initial success. By experiencing mistakes and fixing them to develop a solid business model that franchisees can replicate, the franchisor has developed and protected the brand and the systems that the franchisee can license and use in its business.

The franchisee is acquiring the right to use the brand and the systems to get started much faster and with much stronger resources than he could on his own, and that right has considerable value. Essentially, to be a franchisee is to be in business *for* but not *by* yourself. The franchisor benefits in offering this opportunity to a franchisee because it helps offset past, current, and future investments in the brand and in the operating systems. When done right, franchising benefits both the company, which wants to expand geographically, and the franchisee, who gets to learn the business and execute the model at the local level.

This book will help you evaluate whether franchising can be a great option for you to cost-effectively expand your business. In addition, once you establish that your business is right for franchising, *Grow Smart, Risk Less* will guide you step-by-step through leveraging franchising as a proven expansion vehicle. Many of the specifics and examples are based upon my hands-on experience as a franchisor of a service business.

However, the generalities of the steps that need to be taken to franchise and the order of those steps are common to all franchise concepts and will apply in some way, shape, manner, or form for every franchisor. You will need to be properly capitalized, you will need a franchise disclosure document, you will need to build a team, you will need to define a franchise sales process, and you will need to build a mutually productive culture where you and your franchisees can win.

I have focused on the sequential steps that are characteristic of franchising in general and have elaborated on the areas that can have the biggest impact on success, namely, the internal and external teams, the culture, the technology, and the major goals and accountabilities. Beyond those common components, you also must understand the specific characteristics of your business or industry. For example, retail, hospitality, and food concepts will have real estate considerations and different territory definitions, as well as unit economic metrics and processes that are unique to each business. Some of the steps and best practices will apply to you and your business; other steps may not apply or will require modifications. One key to franchising is that "one size does not fit all." You must decide what will work for you. You also need to know where to go for more information, such as the International Franchise Association, as you drill deeper into your industry-specific issues. A list of resources can be found at the end of this book.

You have spent years getting to this point in your business, and now you have the information to evaluate whether franchising is the right vehicle for you to leverage those years of investment to dramatically grow your business. It took us one full year, from the day we started evaluating franchising as a way to provide our services to more families to the day we sold our first franchise. A recommended timeline to work through the developmental stages is provided in the chart below.

RECOMMENDED TIMELINE TO LAUNCH
From Contemplation to Franchise Launch

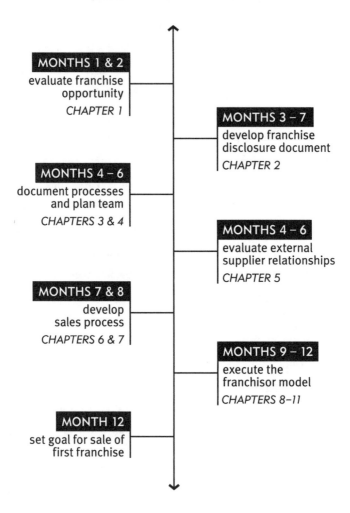

MONTHS 1 & 2
evaluate franchise
opportunity
CHAPTER 1

MONTHS 3 – 7
develop franchise
disclosure document
CHAPTER 2

MONTHS 4 – 6
document processes
and plan team
CHAPTERS 3 & 4

MONTHS 4 – 6
evaluate external
supplier relationships
CHAPTER 5

MONTHS 7 & 8
develop
sales process
CHAPTERS 6 & 7

MONTHS 9 – 12
execute the
franchisor model
CHAPTERS 8–11

MONTH 12
set goal for sale of
first franchise

Section 1 (chapters 1 and 2) walks you through evaluating the franchise opportunity, documenting your processes, joining the relevant associations, attending the necessary events, and preparing your franchise offering so franchisees can evaluate the opportunity to join you. Section 2 (chapters 3 through 5) walks you through the importance of defining the company's vision and culture and the importance of building your internal and external teams from the beginning. It provides a reference guide for the future on how to continue to build out your teams over time. The material in section 3 (chapters 6 and 7) will assist you in selecting the right franchisees and, once you have your franchise offering completed, selling them. Section 4 (chapters 8 through 11) is all about execution and how to be a franchisor. Section 5 (chapters 12 and 13) is about understanding your brand and customers and the relevance they have to building and maintaining a strong foundation for growth and success.

I recommend that you read the book all the way through and then come back to the individual sections at the appropriate time. Use them as a guide to help you determine what to do and what to avoid at each critical stage. The first section lays a needed foundation—with an array of legal, financial, and franchise terms—so hang in there until section 2, because the rest of the book is filled with meatier and more enjoyable topics such as building a team, creating a culture, and building a successful business model for you and your franchisees.

You are entering an exciting time as you evolve your leadership and grow your business from a successful local one to a larger regional, national, or international brand. You had the passion, skills, and determination to get you here. Yes, you will need to learn new things to grow your business through franchising, but you can do it. You will be the ambassador within your organization who will set the tone and the passion for the huge opportunity that franchising can provide when it is done well and with absolute commitment to the interdependent relationship with your franchisees.

When we chose to franchise BrightStar, we could have invested $500,000 in opening three more company-owned locations, or in establishing the franchise platform that has opened over 200 locations in the United States and two locations in Canada in just five years. The franchising model changed our $3 million revenue, two-location business with under $400,000 in annual profit, into a franchise system with more than $100 million in system-wide sales and more than $3 million in annual profit, with built-in growth potential the longer our franchisees are open. Read *Grow Smart, Risk Less* to build your own possibilities for the future!

SECTION 1

EVALUATING THE PLAN

CHAPTER 1

Is Your Concept Franchise Worthy?

You have a great local business. You know you have a product or service that your customers want. Eventually there comes a point when you begin to wonder how to reach more customers. The traditional approach involves raising capital to allow you to open more locations. True, this approach can grow your brand and allow you to reach more customers, but it also means that expanding your business is all up to you. You will be securing and signing for the debt or outside equity and ultimately signing on the dotted line and taking on the increased risk of expansion.

Another avenue for achieving growth in revenues and customers, with more limited capital and potentially less risk, is through franchising, though many business owners do not consider it. Franchising is a great vehicle to help you reach more customers, promote your brand, and increase your visibility and credibility as a brand. Franchising provides a method for expansion through which you are able to grow smartly by increasing revenues at a steady rate with franchisees that are hand-selected to be ambassadors for your brand.

Both the franchisor and the franchisee benefit from this approach. Franchisees invest capital to grow their business at the local level, but they don't have to spend significant amounts of time and resources to figure out every single aspect of the business. As a franchisor, you are licensing your knowledge, trademarks, and systems to them. In doing so, you will leverage the investments you have already made in your brand and in your systems. In return, you earn a stable revenue stream, normally based upon the revenue results of your franchisees.

Franchising is also a powerful mechanism for accelerating growth. Franchisees provide new sources of passion, ideas, and capital. As you read on, you will learn how to create a culture in which franchisees are working hard to build their local businesses, spreading the word for your brand, and bringing great ideas back to you to make the business model stronger for everyone. Franchising is truly about shared success—growing smart—with less risk than going it alone. Good alone . . . better together.

Several critical components need to be in place before you launch a franchise: a thorough understanding of your industry; sufficient experience in your business; a thorough understanding of prospective franchisees' interest in your model/industry; and the building of a solid, profitable and proven business model. Additional steps to be completed after you decide to franchise and before you actually begin to offer franchises for sale include securing trademarks and setting up a strong legal structure.

Understand Your Industry

The first component to look at in evaluating whether you are ready to franchise your business is your knowledge of your industry. As a business owner, you likely understand the competitive landscape in your local market. In preparing for franchising, it is critically important to understand the industry at a broader and more intimate level. Is the demand for your product(s) or service(s) growing or shrinking? Who are the buyers for your product(s) and service(s) and how are they finding you? The assessment of the demographic trends of customers and the pool of employees needed to meet customer demand will be necessary as you evaluate the opportunity to expand through franchising (and the best geographical areas in which to begin).

A franchisee's decision to invest a large portion of personal wealth is a difficult one and, in many instances, life changing. Franchisees need to feel confident that the franchisor knows what to do. I am amazed, and quite frankly perplexed, by the number of franchisors who begin concepts without having first invested their time and money in company-owned units and who have not expanded to additional locations or territories to ensure that their model could be replicated.

AVOID THIS PITFALL:

Don't try to franchise a business without proving success through your first unit(s).

When I was deciding to become a franchisee in two hotels, my criterion was that the franchisor I invested with would have at least 500 locations, with a majority of them doing well, or would have successful company-owned locations.

Throughout the book, I will stress the importance of company-owned units in building a strong foundation for franchising. All of the benefits of company-owned units that we will touch on—helping to understand the business, helping to understand the impact of changes in the model, building credibility with franchisees when they question actions, etc.—add up so that the sum of the parts (having those units for the specific reason being illustrated) are *much* greater than the whole (having company-owned units simply to generate revenue).

Not all concepts require you, the franchisor, to continue to run the company-owned unit(s) after you begin franchising. Selling the company-owned unit(s) can actually be a way to attract the first franchisee and bring in a large infusion of cash that can be reinvested in launching the franchise system. I think the complexity of the model and the level of change in the industry should influence your decision to keep the units or sell them.

We had two locations when we decided to franchise (and added a third later before selling our second and third locations to franchisees), having taken the time to ensure that our first location could be replicated to a second location and having worked through the challenges and/or customizations needed to expand to additional locations. We decided to keep one company-owned unit because of the rapid changes in healthcare expected over the next 10 years. Rather than have our franchisees try unproven, potentially expensive programs, we believed our unit should serve as the incubator to test new technology, new sales techniques, new marketing programs, and so on. Franchisees are running their businesses and have limited bandwidth for identifying changes to the business model and/or testing new marketing programs. By fully vetting and adapting new ideas in our company-owned unit to determine how to help franchisees implement them with the least disruption to their businesses, we could demonstrate that we were invested in it with them for the long haul and were committed to planning and executing the right strategies to be successful.

The Competition

You have to know how your offering will compare with that of the competition in your industry. Benchmarking your competition is a critical exercise that you will need to repeat annually. At this beginning stage, I recommend that you invest in research. I have developed a strong reliance on FRANdata (see the recommended resources list in Appendix B) to supply the franchise disclosure documents (FDDs) of my competitors each year. I look at how competitors' offerings have changed, how their franchisees are performing, how many units they have added, and how many locations closed. I also look at their audited financial statements to see how the franchisors are performing on such key metrics as revenue per dollar of payroll and earnings before interest, taxes, depreciation, and amortization (EBITDA) as a percentage of revenue.

The extent of the competition will set the bar for how your system needs to perform. In any highly competitive industry, you will need to have compelling evidence that your model is better than the other choices available. We knew we were among the best when we looked at our revenues for our early years compared to our competitors' numbers for theirs (when reviewing their FDD Item 19, which we will discuss further in chapter 1). The performance of our company-owned units was important in attracting the first franchisees to our system. We also understood that we had a unique model because the majority of our competitors serviced only seniors and did not provide skilled medical care; we could tell this from the evaluation of their FDD Item 1 (see Appendix A for a description of each item in the FDD).

The information provided from competitor FDDs allows us to compare our offering from a franchisee's perspective and to glean a sense of the profitability of other franchisors based on their current performance. What is missing is information about competitors' performance in their early days as a franchisor. When we launched our franchise system, we needed to build budgets around what we believed we could do; we needed to demonstrate to our bankers that our assumptions were realistic. Comparing what you expect to do in your first five years as a new franchisor to the eighth, tenth, etc., years of a franchisor competitor's performance is comparing apples to oranges. A valid comparison requires a larger research study and is really where FRANdata excels. So let's look at the study we commissioned and how we used it.

From a market study FRANdata prepared for us, we knew our competitors' ranges of unit growth per year in their first 10 years of operation and the key franchisor profitability statistics. This information allowed us to plot our key goals for years one through five on charts for unit sales, cumulative units, total revenues, royalty revenues, EBITDA, revenue per dollar of payroll, and an estimated level of unit sales per franchisee, along with data points for each competitor to show that our goals were within the range of what was possible in our industry. A lender is more willing to make a loan when you can demonstrate what others in your industry have accomplished.

Review the average unit sales at the franchisee level among competitors. Some franchisors will disclose how their franchisees perform in Item 19 of their FDD. This is a valuable way to keep tabs on your competition and valuable information for prospects evaluating the opportunity. If the franchisee performance information isn't disclosed in the FDD, then all you can do is try to estimate it for the aggregate of all franchisees regardless of how long the franchisees have been open. All you need to calculate the average unit sales are the following pieces of information: Item 20, beginning and ending units for a one-year period (to calculate the average number of units); the royalty percentage from Item 6; and the audited financial statements (particularly the royalty revenue line for that year). Divide the royalty revenue line by the royalty percentage to get system-wide sales, which can be further divided by average units to get the estimated average unit sales per franchisee. You can use the research study to understand what the competitor's metrics are in the current period compared to what they were year by year in their early stages.

TO ESTIMATE THE AVERAGE FRANCHISEE SALES FOR COMPETITORS IF THIS INFORMATION IS NOT DISCLOSED IN ITEM 19 OF THE FDD:

$$\text{SYSTEM-WIDE REVENUES} = \frac{\text{ROYALTY REVENUES}}{\text{ROYALTY RATE}}$$

$$\text{AVG. FRANCHISEE SALES} = \frac{\text{SYSTEM-WIDE REVENUES}}{(\text{ENDING UNIT COUNT} + \text{BEGINNING UNIT COUNT})/2}$$

This is an important number to understand initially as you consider whether to franchise your business, and it will help you become more competitive over time. It is very important to your ability to sell franchises to have a model that is producing among the highest returns in the unit's first, second, and third years compared to your competitors, and then to appropriately disclose the company-owned unit performance in Item 19. If your average revenues per franchisee are less than your competitors' in the aggregate with the above calculation, don't worry. Your competitors have the benefit of having franchisees that have been in business for years: They *should* have higher sales than franchisees that have been in business for a shorter period of time. But also recognize what you need to do to improve those results as your system matures.

Evaluating the competition is a critical component in understanding your industry, but it is not a one-time event. Benchmarking your competition is an important exercise that you should undertake regularly to evaluate your trends (improving or declining) compared to your competitors'. I still thoroughly compare key metrics with my competitors each year as part of the budgeting process. We review the most recent FDD and the audited financial statements of the 10 largest competitors in our industry. If there are publicly traded non-franchise companies in your industry, you should also access and evaluate their information, metrics, and competitive differentiation.

We had solid revenues and were a top performer in terms of royalty dollars per unit when comparing our early years to the competitors' early years. However, in the first four years we lagged behind our competition in the efficiency metric, revenue per dollar of payroll, and in EBITDA as a percentage of revenue. We lagged because we had intentionally made an early decision to invest heavily in staff—well-qualified people and more of them (as further explained in chapter 4). I was willing to invest in the quantity and quality of support, including 15+ years of experience on average for franchisee field support and BrightStart team members (BrightStart is the fast launch team we added in 2009 and is discussed in detail in chapter 9). Of course, this decision was expensive, and I knew that in our early years it would put us behind our competitors in efficiency and in EBITDA, but I believed that it would pay for itself in the long term. By the fourth year we started to outperform the majority of our competitors, and our fifth-year numbers were in the top quartile of our peer group based on our competitive benchmarking analysis. Over time, this early investment in talent more than justified the expense.

By now in the evaluation stage you should be able to determine if your franchisees would have a good opportunity to make money if they followed your model. You should know how your model stacks up on ROI compared to your competitors'. The advantage of taking the time to thoroughly evaluate the competition is that you gather the information on what the competition charges its franchisees in terms of fees—royalties, national ad fund (NAF), technology, and any other fees—that you will need to subtract from your company-owned model results to create a pro forma of what the results for a franchisee would be after these costs are paid to the franchisor, to further validate that this results in a strong return for the franchisee for the level of investment she will make. This analysis also allows you to see the range of the fees charged among your competitors to assist you in determining what you will charge. You will evaluate what the competitors charge as well as evaluate what creates a win-win financial model for the franchisees and franchisor in the amounts charged.

During our evaluation we were able to see that the majority of our industry charged a 5 percent royalty, so we chose this as well after evaluating that this fee level should allow the franchisees and BrightStar to make acceptable levels of return for our investments. We added a 6 percent royalty on national account business because we saw an opportunity to build a team that would develop contracts on our franchisees' behalf and charge a slightly higher royalty to offset our costs to develop and maintain this opportunity for our franchisees. Likewise, we were able to see a variety of NAF fees charged, and while many were lower than what we chose, we believed that we could add more value to our franchisees in leveraging the purchasing power of the whole system by handling more advertising, media, and public relations and the corresponding promotion that an NAF provides. Based on that belief, we chose a rate among the highest in our industry. Lastly, we were able to see that nearly every competitor required its franchisees to purchase technology through a third party and that the franchisors did not have the competitive advantage of technology and the innovation that comes from owning their own technology. We were able to review the technology fees charged for out-of-the-box technology solutions and used this information to set the technology fee that we would charge to partially cover our costs and allow us to continue to innovate.

Strong Customer Demand for Products and Services

Another component of understanding your industry is to keep abreast of current (and future) customer demand for your products and services beyond your current geography. Certainly one of the main benefits of franchising is getting your products and services to more markets and thus to more customers. Therefore, it is critical that there is a strong customer demand for the products and services you offer from a macro perspective—people must eat, people will need healthcare, people have pets, etc. You should understand the underlying trends for your industry to ensure that it is growing and that it is also projected to grow over the next 10 to 20 years.

Nearly every industry has strong competition. I believe that healthy competition keeps me (and our company) on our A-game, is good for the industry, and shows me there is demand for what we sell. It is critical that you understand your brand positioning at a local level so you know how to elicit customer demand across a larger geographical reach. Are you the lowest-cost, highest-service, or best-quality provider in the market? You will need a unique differentiation to best exploit the market opportunity through franchising. Assess what has differentiated you locally and compare that to the national competitors in your sector to accurately establish that you have a compelling differentiation nationally. This may require exploration on how to add features and benefits to your offering so that your market differentiation is secured and recognized at a broader level.

Understand Prospective Franchisees

In addition to understanding whether customers want and are willing to pay for your services, you must evaluate the interest of prospective franchisees in buying your concept rather than another's. Obviously the business model must deliver adequate returns (and we will look at this in the next section), but the prospective franchisee must want it. It has to be a better/unique/more sustainable franchise solution than what is currently being offered. In many instances, this point can be defined as ROI and the quality-of-life returns for the target franchisee.

The prospective franchisee must see the value of what you have to offer, for which he will pay a fee up front (defined as initial franchise fees) and a recurring fee over time—usually as a percentage of his revenues (defined as royalties or license fees). Do you have a recognizable brand? Do you have proprietary technology? Do you have sales and operations systems that deliver a higher ROI than others? Do you have a leadership and/or vision advantage? Do you have strategic vendor or customer contract relationships? You need to demonstrate an ability to deliver superior processes, support, and leadership to allow franchisees to get to breakeven significantly faster than they would do on their own (to justify the initial franchise fees and the royalties) and faster than other franchisors for them to select your franchise rather than doing it on their own or with another franchisor.

In addition to the financial return and customer demand that must be in place, you need to see if franchisees want to be in the business of selling what customers want. You need to know if other franchisors in your sector are growing, because it will show you whether or not franchisees are interested in that particular industry segment. For example, look at the doggie waste pick-up business. There is clearly a market from a customer demand perspective, as demonstrated by the Humane Society statistics citing that 77.5 million people in the United States own dogs and that 39 percent of U.S. households own at least one dog. Yet despite good unit economics, this franchise sector is generally not growing at a rate that reflects customer demand. Could it be that people just don't envision themselves in a business where they are cleaning up dog waste for a living? Customer demand and franchisee interest are both necessary components to assessing the future potential of your concept.

Build a Solid Business Model

Your experience in your own business and in becoming an expert in executing your own business model provides a strong foundation with which to begin a successful franchise journey. It is not enough, though, for you to make money running a company-owned model. You must take that knowledge and adjust your results for the additional costs a franchisee will have in licensing your brand, your technology, your systems, and your processes. You must prove that the business can be successful with average performers and not only exceptional performers like you.

The business model must be assessed from both the franchisor and the franchisee vantage point to ensure that both parties can make reasonable

ROIs. If you have company-owned units, this is a much easier exercise. You can take the results from your first through fifth years (or fewer, if you have had your locations less than five years) and model the results for a franchisee in the same business with the adjustments that a franchisee would incur, such as NAF charges, system fees, royalties, and hiring and training employees.

Next, you will want to build a spreadsheet to review what the franchisee results would be at various levels of performance in revenues, or contact us at www.growsmartriskless.com and input the code word GROWSMART to access a template to help you with this evaluation. It is helpful to evaluate the results for a range of revenue scenarios—based upon a 25 percent under-performance through a 25 percent over-performance (or 75–125 percent of targeted revenues)—to see what the franchisee's results would be at certain revenue levels that are 75–125 percent of those achieved by the company-owned model. When looking at our system and at new concepts, and when mentoring, I assume that a franchisee puts up 30–40 percent of the capital for the launch of a franchise. I also assume that the franchisee could earn an acceptable level of return by the third year (generally 15 percent or more of capital investment) if handling one of the full-time roles (i.e., not hiring someone else to do it) and after covering debt service. As noted earlier, you may need to make adjustments to this evaluation based on your business and your industry.

This analysis is assessing reasonable returns for the franchisees while they are running their business, and the value of their business when they decide to sell it is *incremental* to reward their "sweat equity." In the current economic environment, I believe the most successful models are able to produce a reasonable return for the capital invested, deliver a reasonable salary by the third year if the owner is working full-time in the business, and create an opportunity for wealth for a franchisee's retirement when the business is sold at a later date. Of course, this analysis is based on the assumption that the franchisee follows the business model to achieve at least 75 percent of past results. I like to see a franchisee in a position to take a reasonable salary and/or a distribution at some point beginning in year two.

All franchisees have different expectations for the time period in which they should begin making money and the amount of money they want or need to make to achieve an adequate return. Some are looking to replace their salary (and that could be a wide range from $30,000 to hundreds of thousands of dollars per year). Industries, as well, have different expectations of return, based on the level of the investment. The level of expected return will also vary if the franchisee will be an investor (and is therefore able to keep her existing job) or an owner-operator (and must commit full-time to the business she is buying), and if there is real estate involved (and if the franchisee buys it or leases it back to or from the franchisor). Also, prospective franchisees in different industries will have different pressure points in evaluating the opportunity: For example, restaurant investors may be focused on the sales-to-investment ratio and the combined costs of goods (food and labor costs). Different industries will have different metrics; you need to know yours and demonstrate that you are a top performer as a new entrant to attract franchisees.

Generally, investor franchisees (rather than owner-operators) are willing to wait longer for investment recovery. Today, owner-operators are becoming less patient than in the past and expect a quicker return, though I think the new economy is creating more realistic expectations as to the level of returns, just as the employment market has lowered expectations for salaries and benefits. From my networking in the franchising industry, I deduce that there is a common viewpoint that many owner-operators, particularly those in service industries, are looking for replacement income quicker, and this is important to understand in evaluating how strong your business model is. These owner-operators are looking for concepts that have an opportunity to deliver breakeven levels by the end of the first year or so, replacement income in year two, and recovered cash by the end of year three. Again, these are generalities and will vary when the franchisee is buying capital assets, buildings, equipment, etc.

There are a few good consulting groups (ask around and see who is active in the International Franchise Association before choosing) to assist in launching a franchise system. However, it is critical that a feasibility analysis be completed *first*, prior to spending money to launch a franchise system. When I hear a new franchisor talk about paying a consultant more than $100,000 to launch a system and there was not a thorough feasibility analysis early on (at a fraction of the price), I see a red flag. That franchisor doesn't know with any certainty whether his franchisees will make money according to his business model; he doesn't know how the ROI on his offering compares to that of his competition; and he doesn't know if he is adequately capitalized until the franchise entity reaches royalty self-sufficiency. More often than not, new franchisors don't even know what "royalty self-sufficiency" means (we will discuss that in chapter 8). Even though these are some of the most important questions new franchisors need to have answered, the consulting group typically gives them only an FDD or related franchise documentation, an operations manual, and marketing materials. The consultant may never work with the new franchisor on a detailed analysis of these critical financial factors. Rather, the consultant's work product will be founded on the assumption that the new franchisor has the answers and that they are favorable. Why spend such a large sum of money without first ensuring that the concept is franchise worthy? This is your responsibility, so own it.

Establishing the Legal Foundation

Once you are confident in your ability to franchise, you need to lay a strong legal foundation by protecting your trademarks beyond your local market and by establishing the legal structure from which to launch the franchise.

Securing Trademarks

As you think about expanding, it is critical that you protect your brand. The first step is to hire an intellectual property attorney to perform a search with the U.S. Patent and Trademark Office (PTO) to ensure that your name or mark is not being used elsewhere and that you can obtain the rights to use it nationally. It would be a disaster to begin to expand into other markets and then find out that you do not have the legal right to use your name or mark in that market. You could be sued for using the name of an already established business.

As a small business owner, you may think that you already have a lot of brand equity, but that equity won't go far if you are unable to protect it and other businesses own names, URLs, and intellectual property that is similar to your own (and quite possibly trademark protected).

If you are unable to get the trademark rights for your business's name, you will need to invest in creating another brand before franchising. When we started our company-owned location in 2002, our name was very generic (24-7 HealthCare Solutions). We made a $40,000 investment in 2004 to create a brand for which we could secure trademark rights and which customers would remember. We already had loyalty to our services and company, but we knew we needed to invest in building and protecting a brand. In addition to the $40,000 we spent to create the initial BrightStar brand, we spent $30,000 to have another company withdraw their PTO application for "BrightStar Recruiters" and about $10,000 in PTO filing fees.

AVOID THIS PITFALL:

Avoid generic branding, like what we had in the beginning, in favor of spending the money for a professional branding firm to help you create a brand identity that embodies your core market differentiators and/or your brand's customer promise.

You should own the website addresses, or URLs, for your brand, and someone in the company should have an eye on ensuring that the ownership rights do not lapse. Your attorney should offer monitoring services to ensure that trademarks and URLs are renewed on a regular basis (although it's probably good backup to assign this task to an in-house staff person too). You also want to think about securing additional URLs that encompass your brand, such as "namefranchise.com" and "namefranchising.com," so you have them for the future franchise sales website.

BRIGHT IDEA:

I recommend investing in URLs that others may try to buy if you don't, such as "name-sucks.com," "name.net," "name.org," etc. The costs are minimal and help to protect your brand from derogatory sites or brand confusion in the market.

Finally, if you have developed your own technology that your franchisees will use, I recommend consulting with a patent attorney to see if what you have built can be protected. The technology will need to be unique, but this can be a smart investment to protect against franchise prospects who may be your competitors in disguise.

Legal Structure

Franchising has many legal considerations. In this section we will focus on establishing the appropriate legal entity for the franchisor, and then in chapter 2 we will review the preparing and filing of the FDD. The areas that are common in setting up all business entities—such as acquiring a federal employer identification number (FEIN), determining the entity type, and then preparing the bylaws, articles of incorporation, and/or the operating agreement—are excluded from this section, as these are not unique to franchising and were steps you had to undertake in the formation of your company-owned legal entity.

I am often amazed by the risks that franchisors take by leaving their company-owned business in the same legal entity that they use for their franchise system. I would not want to risk all the future potential of my franchise system to an unhappy customer or employee of my company-owned unit. We separated our company-owned entity from our franchise system from the beginning.

That being said, however, we did make a change in early 2010 to further separate our company-owned entity into two entities. After reviewing our original trademarks, we realized that the entity not only owned the trademarks but also owned and operated the company-owned locations. At that point, we made the investment to move the intellectual property into a separate entity for its protection and then formed a new entity for the company-owned operations.

BRIGHT IDEA:

Regardless of the size of your franchise system, the review of where your intellectual property is held and the separation of it from company-owned operations and from franchise operations is a worthy exercise to undertake with your board of advisors and attorney.

Closing Thoughts

You have spent years, passionate energy, and financial resources building a successful business. You are ready to expand and have begun to evaluate whether franchising can be a way to leverage your investments up to this point.

In this chapter, you learned how important understanding your industry and your business experience to date will be in launching a successful franchise system. Franchising builds upon your solid business model and customer demand for your goods and services. That said, the important point here is that *franchising is a new business.* We went from being only in the healthcare business to also being in the franchise business.

Franchising provides a low-risk and proven model for expansion for both the franchisor and the franchisee when the model is financially strong and executed properly with the right foundation. You have the tools to evaluate the investment a franchisee will make and to compare that with what your competition offers. Once you have determined that you have a model that can deliver financial success for the franchisor and the franchisee, you will want to invest in securing your intellectual property and building a solid legal structure.

Growth through franchising will require you to learn new skills and to adapt a new approach, which we will discuss throughout the book. Leading franchisees is different from leading employees: The former requires the ability to manage a business, which runs more on influence, than does the latter, which is more a matter of command and control.

. . .

As a final step in your evaluation, you can also access a 360-degree assessment tool at www.growsmartriskless.com to help you interview key employees, customers, suppliers, other stakeholders, and—most important—target investors about the potential to replicate the model for others.

Now that you've completed your assessment and determined that you have a business concept worthy of franchising, it's time to get further educated about franchising, to secure capital, and to prepare your FDD. Continue on to chapter 2 for tips on each of these areas.

CHAPTER 2

Your Franchise Meets the Test—

Now What?

Congratulations! You are confident that your concept is franchise worthy! Or, if it isn't but you are still reading on, it's never too late to retool your model—to invest the time and financial resources to improve your system. In fact, we all have to keep our concepts fresh, because customers' demands change and your competitors won't sit still.

In this chapter you will learn the fundamentals of how to prepare yourself and your organization for franchising. Great resources are available to help you navigate the learning curve at the beginning of this journey as well as to keep you applying best practices for continual improvement as a franchisor.

Once we have you steeped in learning and the available resources that can enable you to be a world-class franchisor, we will explore the capital needed to launch a franchise system. With further knowledge and capital in place, it is time to look at how you will prepare your own franchise disclosure statement (FDD) for the launch of your franchise system.

Become a Student of Franchising

If you intend to go into the business of franchising, you must learn and understand what it means to be a *good* franchisor. The founder must be "all in" as a leader, a franchisor, a brand champion, a transparent communicator with integrity, and a relationship builder. You can be excellent at delivering your product or service *and* be an unskilled franchisor; in this case, everyone loses—you and the franchisees that want to join and follow you. I don't believe franchising is merely a distribution model or solely an expansion strategy. It's *a business unto itself.* When you understand that, then you recognize that franchising is also *an industry unto itself.* For example, BrightStar operates in two industries—healthcare and franchising.

Furthering your education about franchising encompasses three equally important areas: associations, mentors, and your franchise communication network. First, you need to join associations and attend as many franchise-focused events as possible. Second, you'll want to find someone who can mentor you during the first months you are franchising your business. And third, you'll want to keep your franchisees informed about franchise trends to ensure the greatest success for everyone.

Active Participation in the Franchise Industry

If you are new to franchising, the good news is that lots of resources are available to you as a student. Primary among them is the International Franchise Association (IFA), an association dedicated to helping franchisors and franchisees learn and constantly improve their knowledge and understanding of franchising. You will soon get to the point where you know the basics and have built a few key relationships with other franchisors and needed suppliers. Within one year of becoming active in IFA, for example, I obtained my designation as a Certified Franchise Executive (CFE), had an array of mentors available to me, and had formed a board of advisors made up of accomplished franchise leaders and suppliers. I was learning about franchising while I was also building my franchise. Often, the best learning happens when you can ask specific questions and apply the teaching to real-life situations.

BRIGHT IDEA:

Begin your discovery and become a student of franchising while you are following the path to launching and growing your franchise system.

Attend two or three events per year to learn and network. The more events you attend, the more people you meet. Someone will always welcome you and take you under his wing. I highly recommend attending the IFA's Annual Convention and Franchise Update Media Group's annual Franchise Leadership & Development Conference. A third great event for new franchisors is the Emerging Franchisor Conference sponsored by Nova Southeastern University each November in Fort Lauderdale. If you have been in franchising but just haven't been able to get the value you need thus far, make a commitment for a year to attend these great educational and networking events.

International Franchise Association

The International Franchise Association is the oldest and largest organization representing franchising worldwide. IFA's mission is to protect, enhance, and promote franchising through government relations, media relations, and professional development programs. IFA offers the following development opportunities:

+ a remarkable low-cost/high-value introductory two-year membership;
+ a Certified Franchise Executive program to enhance the professionalism of franchising by certifying the highest standards of quality training and education and by helping franchisors gain the knowledge they need to lead a world-class franchise organization;
+ the FranShip program, through which you can access a mentor; and

✦ the FranGuard program, held throughout the year, where you can learn about the legal and business aspects of compliance in the franchise sales process.

Plan ahead and prepare for IFA's annual convention by selecting the educational and roundtable session topics that are the most critical to you at the time. Make note of the speakers and table hosts for the sessions you attend and try to meet them. My strategy is to identify one or two areas in which I need to learn multiple best practices. For example, in 2006 and 2007, I focused on how to plan my first franchisee conference, which we held in June 2007. In 2007 and 2008, I focused on establishing our Franchise Advisory Council. In 2009 and 2010, I focused on international expansion—where to go and not to go first, how to support, how to structure, etc. In each case I learned what to avoid and took the business card of a few experts to contact after I got home. When I was able to execute on what I learned, it was evident that the time and money invested in attending the conference had paid huge dividends. Bear in mind that these conventions are large and can be a bit overwhelming. Each year, focus on and prioritize a topic or two, getting to know three to five new people really well (rather than getting the business cards of 200 people and remembering none of them), and getting to know and evaluate two or three potential new suppliers.

Another way the IFA can help you is through the FranPAC, a political action committee. FranPAC represents the industry and our very livelihood against proposed onerous legislation and regulation that could negatively impact the cost of doing business. Your contributions will support pro-business candidates for federal office who understand the benefits of a climate favorable to franchising. Anyone who benefits from franchising should contribute to the FranPAC—$1 a day would get you their "365" pin to wear proudly. Once you have supported the FranPAC, subscribe to the briefs on the key issues to watch, contact your representatives (the IFA provides the tools on the website to do that quickly and easily), and attend the annual Public Affairs Conference, where more than 500 franchisors and franchisees meet with their representatives to educate them on proposed legislation that we need them to support or oppose.

AVOID THIS PITFALL:

Meeting those who are well respected within IFA circles would have saved me $75,000 in legal fees paid to a big national law firm and $25,000 paid to a big national public relations firm that didn't understand franchising.

As you begin to get your sea legs, get more involved by joining IFA committees—which is another great way to meet people in smaller groups and begin giving back to the association that will give you so much.

When I think about $2,200 for a two-year membership in the IFA and a conference registration, plus travel costs to the conferences, it is small change compared to the cost of picking the wrong lawyer and the wrong PR firm.

Franchise Update Media Group's Leadership & Development Conference

This annual event for franchisors only focuses on two key areas: growing the number of new franchisees and leadership. New franchisors can gain insight from peers who are leaders in the franchise industry into what lead-generation tools and technology are working the best. Franchise Update's mission, as they see it, is as follows: "Increase Leads. Boost Sales. Grow Your Brand."

The conference offers 25 educational sessions focused on franchise sales, marketing, and development; five in-depth pre-conference power sessions; and revealing research, such as their "Annual Franchise Development Report."

In addition, there is an all-day Franchise CEO Summit exclusively for CEOs and presidents that provides a private, interactive environment in which franchise CEOs can solve tough issues, exchange ideas, develop best practices, and discover how to respond to make-or-break decisions through strategic business conversations that typically wouldn't, or simply couldn't, take place anywhere else. The CEO Summit is designed to help you achieve your goal of building a truly great company.

The access to information and benchmarking data and the ability to develop relationships with industry leaders make this a "must attend" event for me every year. It is the only venue with a solid focus on growth in the number of franchisees and how to achieve that singular goal.

Executive Leadership Conference

A third conference for the leaders of franchise companies is my favorite of the year. It is the IFA's Executive Leadership Conference (ELC), where you have the rare opportunity to interact in an intimate setting with business leaders, futurists, economists, and notable professors. In your first couple of years, you will want to strongly consider attending Nova's Emerging Franchisor Conference and then, as you move beyond the launch stage of your franchise system, the ELC will provide the networking and ideas to help evolve your system to the next level.

Find a Mentor

Franchising is unique. In no other industry will you find so many who are willing to share so much and where networking turns into deep friendships. I encourage you to seek out well-known experts in the industry as mentors at particular points in time to help you with your most important objectives. You can identify the experts by attending educational sessions at conferences and selecting those speakers who have a compelling message and style from which you could benefit. I have gone to experts for advice and then, as I implemented the techniques they suggested, they've helped me with challenges or questions I had along the way. Experts are busy, so I work around their schedules and I try to honor a start and a stop date so they know my request for their mentorship is not indefinite.

I met my first mentor, Kurt Landwehr, in Atlanta at the Franchise Update Media Group's Franchise Leadership & Development Conference in September 2006. I attended an all-day session conducted by Kurt, Tom Wood, and Brian Schnell, and though I learned a lot about franchise sales, I realized I needed to learn a lot more. I tracked Kurt down and asked if he would mentor me to help me build our sales process. He said he had limited time during the day but would spend his Thursday evenings and Saturday mornings for a few months with me. I meticulously took notes on everything he said during each phone conversation we had. We would not have sold fifteen units in the first year without him. He and I have continued as friends over the years, and Kurt even ran our sales department for a year until we filled the role on-site. Having a mentor to go to for advice and coaching really accelerates the learning curve. While the scheduled time may subside as your knowledge in an area increases, that mentor is always there to go back to when you need a sounding board. I find my mentors to be a safety net as I need a breakthrough in a particular area or function within our organization.

Your Franchisees Need to Be Educated Too

The more you learn about franchising as your system grows, the more important it will be to educate your franchisees. Franchisees always benefit from being informed. One way to provide them with information is to register your entire system to receive communications from the IFA, particularly the legislative briefs. Beginning in late 2008, I began bringing my top-performing multi-unit franchisee to the Public Affairs Conference to see his representatives and participate in the IFA Franchisee Forum (yes, I paid for his travel). In 2010, I also began paying for him to attend the IFA Annual Convention. I think active participation by franchisees—not just ours, but those of all systems—is their responsibility. It is our collective system, and many great ideas come from franchisees and corporate working together to accomplish more.

Another benefit of keeping franchisees informed is that they will be able to compare the range of support across the franchising industry. What better way is there for them to really appreciate how well their system works or how strong or lacking their support level is? I like the perspective my corporate team and my franchisees gain annually: It is one thing for me to say how strong our support is, and another to actually show doubters how rare it is to have a franchisor invest in a support infrastructure like BrightStar's.

Secure Capital

As is true for franchisees, the number one failure for franchisors is under-capitalization. This section will help you get past that danger point.

It is very important to ensure you have enough capital to launch *and* enough capital to invest in support until recurring revenues of royalties can cover your overhead. Many franchisors make a big mistake in calculating only the amount they need to launch, wrongly assuming that the amount they collect from selling franchises in initial franchise fees will cover overhead. New franchisors often assume that they can grow their company using other people's money, but often the franchise fee revenues do not fund the necessary infrastructure, leaving the emerging franchisor scrambling. If you are not sitting on a cash war chest of $500,000, you may run out of cash before you achieve the point of royalty self-sufficiency. (In chapter 8, I discuss royalty self-sufficiency—the point at which royalties paid by franchisees cover the overhead costs of the franchisor—in much more detail.)

BRIGHT IDEA:

You need to understand how to assess the initial capital needed to launch the franchise and to sustain it to the point of royalty self-sufficiency.

Once you have estimated the amount of money needed, you need to prepare the information required in order for you to access financing through your bank. Let's walk through both of these key aspects of securing capital in greater detail.

Assess Capital Requirements

Remember, you must consider not only the amount of financing needed to launch the franchise system, but also the cumulative amount you will need until the franchise becomes royalty self-sufficient. You will learn as you go through these chapters about all the areas to consider in terms of the personnel to hire and when to hire them, as well as the opportunities to use suppliers for certain projects to delay the hiring of personnel. The good news is that by reading this book and following the steps included, you can understand how to avoid some of the pitfalls we encountered.

We estimated we needed to invest $300,000 to launch the franchise and sustain it until the point of royalty self-sufficiency. I contributed $100,000 of our own money and accessed $200,000 in debt financing. We were about 18 months in when the cash began to get painfully tight.

We actually needed $500,000, so we thought we had underestimated. It turned out, however, that we had a cash drain problem.

We had overspent during those 18 months on unnecessary or ill-advised hiring: at least $100,000 on legal and public relations firms not active in IFA; $50,000 for salaried employees to do work that contracted consultants could have done, particularly franchise training; and $50,000 to $75,000 for outside help in the first year to handle franchise sales when that role really belonged to a founder or key executive. (Ultimately, we had to involve either my husband or me in every franchise sale, so hiring personnel for this position was unnecessary.) Add up those overages and you see that our initial estimate of $300,000 would have been adequate if we had known then what we know now. You may avoid our pitfalls by reading this book, but you should still plan on $100,000 to $200,000 in additional cash reserves—over and above what your financial model shows you need to fund your franchise through the point of royalty self-sufficiency—as you find new pitfalls that might put you in the position to fumble on the five-yard line.

Access Capital

Among the sources of capital you'll want to consider when setting up your franchise are these: investing the profits from your company-owned units in the new entity that will franchise; borrowing from a bank; borrowing money through a government program in your state; or borrowing money from friends and/or family. The following section will walk you through how to pursue capital from these sources.

BORROWING FROM BANKS

You will always need more capital than you think. Although the lessons I share in this book could save you many thousands of dollars, you may have to learn new lessons on your own that will result in unexpected costs and the need to borrow. The capital markets have gotten tighter, but there is still money available.

Banks review lots of requests, and they are going to be more inclined to loan to those who make their job easier by anticipating their questions and concerns as to how their loan will be repaid. In our first business plan for franchising, we intended to sell 10 franchises in the first year, another 25 in the second year, 40 in the third year, and about 50 each year in the fourth and fifth years. Naturally, the bank questioned how we would sell 10 franchises in a year without any experience. As I discussed in chapter 1, we had thoroughly researched our competitors and we were prepared to convince the bank that we would be able to meet our goal.

You will need to have great market research on your industry sector and performance compared to your peers; you will need to exert strong confidence in your abilities to achieve the results in your business plan and to repay the loan; and you will need to have skin in the game. Expect to give a personal guaranty for the loan, including securing the franchising entity loan with the assets of the company-owned entity. Also, see how much of the profit of the company-owned entity can be distributed or loaned (consult your legal and tax advisors for advice) to the franchising entity without weakening the former in the effort to help the latter launch and grow.

You will want to be thoroughly prepared before you meet with the bank. The key items to include in your package are these: a full business plan; financial statements for the first five years, including a statement of cash flow; and the competitive analysis on your industry to show that your assumptions for unit sales by year, royalty revenues per year and per unit, and earnings as a percentage of revenue are within the ranges of what has occurred historically in the industry.

BORROWING THROUGH A GOVERNMENT PROGRAM

I scoured all the possible government programs, concentrating on ones that were available to women-owned businesses, and sure enough, in Illinois I found a program that would loan up to $200,000. I had to put in $100,000, which I had planned to do anyway, and I had to create 20 jobs during the five-year loan term ($10,000 per job). You'll be amazed by the number of resources that may be available within your state, especially if your company-owned units are performing well.

I met with the bankers who would underwrite the state program. I prepared binders with a presentation and tabs for five-year projections of income statements, balance sheets, and, most important, cash flows. I rehearsed the presentation over and over and then, on the big day, went through it from memory. I was nervous, but just like the deodorant commercial, I didn't let them see me sweat. I got the loan. Although the lending climate is different as of this writing, I could get funded again if I spent the same time on market research and preparation. I might need to pitch 10 banks before finding a lender, but I would get one. And so can you.

OTHER SOURCES OF CAPITAL

Remember how I underestimated the money we needed by $200,000? That was a hard moment, but I knew we would ultimately make it. We had to access more capital and really build, or entrench and stall growth. Knowing that the 12 franchisees were with us because of their belief in the vision of our future—which meant growing, not going home defeated—we tabled our pride and asked my husband's parents for a loan of $200,000. It was a big chunk, and I was so ashamed to ask them that I requested J.D. to ask his mom and dad without me being by his side for support.

They agreed to help us. My pride had me structuring the one-year loan with 14 percent interest (to match their returns in the market, since they had to pull out the money to loan to us). We were able to pay it back in 11 months, using franchising and the company-owned operations to do it. We will always be grateful that they stood by us. Receiving financial help from family members is humbling and is something that stays with you, grounds you, and drives you to never have to repeat the experience.

This experience encouraged us over the years to empathize with franchisees that were struggling with proper capitalization. In a few instances, we cosigned loans for four franchisees and loaned money outright to three. You won't be able to help out everyone in need, of course. If you reach a point where you can help out franchisees, be sure to limit assistance to those who are absolutely following the model and just need a temporary helping hand. Our experience is more typical than many may realize—the first 12 to 18 months in any business is when "cash is king" and things are tight. Everything is on the line financially, and you must match it with a positive, high-energy attitude. You need to "be in it for the right reasons, use all of the available tools, and be in it to win it," to borrow a line from our president of BrightStar Care.

Making it to the third year in business is reaching the "sweet spot," that is, the point where, if you have been diligent in building your system and doing the right thing during your first two years, you should know from your strong indicators that you can make it. Generally the indicators fall into two areas and are true for both franchisors and franchisees: (1) Average unit sales are on par with your peers; and (2) your franchisees are satisfied (measured by two-thirds franchisee satisfaction, per a survey administered by a third party that we will discuss more in chapter 10) and/or your customers are satisfied (measured by a net promoter score that we will discuss more in chapter 12).

Prepare Your Franchise Disclosure Document

Now, with a solid business model, market opportunity, secured intellectual property, and capital in place, it is time for you to invest in a great franchise attorney and prepare your franchise disclosure document (FDD) so that you can begin screening potential franchisees to join your system. The work up until now has prepared you for the launch. It is time to begin growing your franchise system, and the FDD is one of the first steps in the official launching process.

As you build your franchise program, you will learn that franchising is regulated in different respects at both the federal and the state levels. One aspect of the regulatory environment for franchisors is the presale requirements that apply to the offer and sale of franchises. The FDD is the disclosure document that is required by the Federal Trade Commission and those states that regulate the offer and sale of franchises. The FDD serves a critical purpose in the franchise sales process, as it is intended to provide a prospective franchisee with the essential information that will allow the prospect to make an informed decision about the franchise opportunity and business. Beyond the disclosures required by franchise laws, the FDD includes a copy of the franchise agreement and all exhibits that a prospective franchisee must sign as part of joining the franchise system. In addition to the FDD requirements, you will need to understand many other legal aspects that apply to franchising. As you can imagine, your decision on whom to use as franchise counsel is an important one.

At the IFA convention you will find representatives from many great law firms that have been active with the IFA for years. There is no harm in interviewing a few law firms and negotiating for a flat fee to prepare the FDD. You may get a recommendation from those you meet at franchising events or from a board member. That's how I found our second lawyer,

Lane Fisher of Fisher & Zucker, LLC, who helped us improve on our first franchise disclosure document.

BRIGHT IDEA:

When you begin researching a law firm, leverage the most powerful resources in franchising—the IFA and its members and connections.

As we continued to grow, and as healthcare disclosure items and healthcare state and federal regulations began changing rapidly, we needed a larger law firm that handled franchising and trademarks *and* that had a dedicated healthcare practice. I prefer working with well-connected, smaller firms, because I want strong relationships with those with whom I do business (I'm a hugger!), but in a regulated industry like healthcare, it's often necessary to go with a larger firm.

Once you have selected an attorney to prepare the franchise disclosure document—ideally on a fixed-fee arrangement, with separate rates for the initial FDD and for renewals—it is time to get ready to prepare your FDD. Some of the work can be done on your own, prior to selecting the attorney. But as you begin working with your franchise lawyer, you will be provided a set of questions to consider in determining what you want in your FDD.

As a place to start preparing and to help you with any insomnia, gather your competitors' FDDs and read through them. Mark the sections you like from each, and then look for areas of difference among the FDDs. Use this research to come up with topics and questions for your attorney and for your advisors to help you discover the pros and cons of each. Researching beforehand will save your attorney time so she can spend the hours allotted to the assignment, thinking through some of the deal points rather than walking you through each of the items in the FDD.

BRIGHT IDEA:
I prefer a fixed-fee arrangement: The attorney should invest time learning your business, understanding your competitors, and determining your preferences in structuring your FDD.

Initial Franchise Disclosure Document

So how do you simplify the process? What steps can you take early to prepare for a smooth initial FDD? Here are my recommendations:

1. Pull the five-year model that you prepared from chapter 1 to assist with the FDD Item 6 and Item 7 inputs.

2. Gather as much information as you have on company-owned operations to populate Item 19, including a full earnings statement and any key statistical information. Some franchisors provide some form of financial performance information to prospects; other franchisors do not. You must decide what is appropriate for you and then work with your franchise attorney and franchise sales team accordingly. For example, for our business, we include in our Item 19 the number of sales calls per period and/or number of customers, dollars per transaction (average ticket), and/or the average length of service per client. I believe a thorough Item 19 is key to an effective sales process because it allows you to share information with prospects and then to ensure that your sales process covers only this information, to avoid any illegal financial performance representations. An illegal financial performance representation can occur if you share financial information about your unit or system performance and that information is not included in Item 19; you can talk only about what is disclosed. For those reasons, you will want to make absolutely certain that you and your team understand the rules (the legal dos and don'ts) regarding

the sharing of financial performance information with prospective franchisees.

3. Gather competitor FDDs and mark the sections in each where you like the language and/or terms.

4. Note the sections in the competitor FDDs that vary from one another and what the options are to consider. Discuss with advisors first and make a list of these areas to discuss with your franchise attorney.

5. Review your company-owned market profile to understand the population areas that clients come from (if retail), where sales calls are made (if service), or for the number of cars driving by (via a traffic study for hospitality) to assist with defining territory size.

Decision Points

What are some of the areas—the decision points—for you to consider long and hard? The following list describes how we evolved our FDD once we learned more in the process. This list also shows how we might do things differently in our future FDD and for future concepts. Each situation will be unique, and what is appropriate for you is something you will discuss with your franchise attorney and other advisors. What follows is merely a list to educate you on the decision points to consider and the areas—along with your specific industry considerations—for you to review concerning what your competitors have chosen (and to assess the strengths and weaknesses in the results of their choices).

1. What type of franchising—single unit, multi-unit, area representation, or area developer—is appropriate for you? We chose to be the direct franchisor here in the United States but have chosen to select master franchisees outside the United States that can provide key support for their sub-franchisees because they understand local customs and laws. In the United States, we also chose to sell single units and/

or multi-units on a development schedule. We were one of the few in our industry selling multi-unit agreements, but we knew that, with a higher investment range, we would attract a buyer who would need this opportunity. (Chapter 7 gives more details on attracting the right buyer to your concept.) I would offer multi-unit agreements again, but likely with smaller territories in certain situations (as discussed in Item 5 below).

BRIGHT IDEA:

In most instances, limit the number of territories per person to two until they have proven themselves with opening the first territory and being at or better than the system average at six months.

Some franchisors have expanded through an area developer or area representation model, whereby the franchisor establishes a three-party franchise model rather than a direct franchisor–franchisee relationship. In this three-party system, the franchise agreement typically is a contract between the franchisee and franchisor, but the area developer/area representative is a third party who also is under contract with the franchisor and performs many of the franchisor's obligations in a specific geographic territory, including franchise sales recruitment, in-store training, and ongoing operational support. Subway and UPS stores are examples of this three-party franchise model.

2. Where will you open and why? Will you take a geographical approach (those with the best demographics concentrated in a few states at the beginning and/or states close to the company-owned locations so that it's easier and less costly to support) or a prospect approach (anywhere that offers a great prospect)? The geography approach makes

a lot more sense and costs less to execute, due to lower travel costs, if you rely on location density. Food concepts all have distribution and supply chain issues, so concentric growth through this geographical approach typically is a best practice. Further, with retail concepts, you want to make customers aware of your brand through visibility of multiple locations. For BrightStar, because we are in a service industry and no one sees our non-retail office space, geography didn't matter to the same degree.

We chose a prospect approach, and even though we did spend the money to pre-map the United States to identify the territories we could develop, in hindsight we could have used the information to potentially delay from the very first stage of development a state in which there were not at least 10 available territories to sell.

AVOID THIS PITFALL:
We could have held off for at least a year in a handful of states and saved money on FDD filing fees and legal complexity, as well as on marketing the franchise opportunity.

Although smaller states may have strong territories and there is no legal reason not to offer and sell in all states right from the beginning, the costs of registering and complying with state franchise laws require certain economies of scale in the first few years of franchising when you are watching every penny.

3. When will you launch the national ad fund (NAF)? You need to decide whether to begin taking contributions from franchisees at inception or at the time of critical mass measured by the number of open units or system-wide sales. We wrote our initial FDD to launch the NAF after we had opened 25 locations, to avoid upsetting franchisees who

might resist paying into it before that critical mass had been reached. Our NAF is set with a floor of $500, or 1 percent of prior month sales, whichever is greater. I would have started it much sooner if I were to do it again because, with search engine optimization and search engine marketing, it is easy to spend the money in markets or ways that will benefit the franchisees.

AVOID THIS PITFALL:

Launching the NAF sooner would have allowed me to hire marketing personnel sooner, which I waited way too long to do. As a result, I paid far more for outside suppliers to do the work.

4. Do you offer protected territories or not? You should evaluate what is in the combined best interests of the franchisees and you as the franchisor. You want to ensure that your choice in defining territories enables the growth in brand awareness and gives end customers access to the goods or services you offer. If your competitors are selling protected territories, it will be nearly impossible for you not to. Protected territories are more common in service industries. I caution you against referring to territories as "exclusive" and to use "protected" instead. "Exclusive" implies to a franchisee that no one will do anything in his territory—regardless of new expansions you have, their inability to perform part of the business model due to licensure, or their compliance with brand standards.

5. What size should your territories be and how are the territories defined—by zip code, by households, by city, or otherwise? I recommend erring on the smaller side of the range of your competitors and then potentially negotiating on the first few if needed and as permitted by franchise laws. Territories should be defined by where 80–90

percent of the customers will be coming from and the size of that area, its demographics, and/or the traffic patterns in the territory of your successful company-owned units. I recommend defining territory sizes with only one factor, not multiple ones. All of our first franchise agreements specified a per-territory minimum population of 200,000; however, because most of our initial franchisees' business was senior care, our secondary territory criterion was a minimum of 30,000 over the age of 65 (2 to 4 times the number designated by most competitors). As we invested in our model to expand into disabled adult care—including the care of veterans, child care, and staffing—that minimum no longer made sense. In some areas of the country there were large territories in which franchisees were not penetrating the sales opportunity.

We studied correlations of territory size to franchisee performance, and found that there was no material correlation in the initial stage of a franchise location (unless a franchisee is willing to invest in multiple salespeople) because a salesperson can realistically cover only 175,000 in average population. With this careful review, we changed territory size definitions to remove the second criterion of 30,000 over 65—the age limitation—and did not see a material change in average unit performances in new territory definitions.

Our decision to change territory size definitions underscores a key point that all franchisors address at different times in their evolution. You will make decisions early on as you launch your franchise program. You then should constantly review some decisions and approaches as you evolve and your business or system changes. Here again, your franchise attorney can help provide you with the necessary flexibility in your franchise documents to enable you to do what is in the best interests of you and the system.

The territory decisions you will consider and the decisions you make are also dependent on your industry. Different industries have unique ways to define territories. Many retail and brick-and-mortar service brands define protected territory according to geography in miles between locations.

6. Are there minimum performance requirements? Are there minimum levels of sales that franchisees must achieve? And if they don't achieve the minimum level, how will they make up for it, or "cure"? You must be able to demonstrate that it is possible to achieve these minimums through company-owned results and, once you have franchisees, that it is possible for the majority of franchisees who are following the model to achieve them. (We will discuss in chapter 10 the importance to the culture of flexibility in applying performance requirements when temporary external factors affect franchisees' ability to achieve them.)

7. What is your philosophy on vendor rebates (needed for the FDD Item 8)? It is more common for franchisors in the food service industry to keep rebates because they do a lot of work on supply chain management. Our philosophy is that we should make our earnings on royalties, so we specifically state in Item 8 that we will not derive any financial benefit from vendor rebates. Although it is legal to receive vendor rebates as long as everything is properly disclosed in your FDD, often there is a cost. Certain franchisees may look at rebates as hidden royalty. The products or services that franchisees buy through franchisor-approved or -required vendors should be available for purchase at terms equal to or better than those offered elsewhere *for the same quality and under the same circumstances,* or the franchisees may revolt when and if sales flatten.

We do, however, disclose in Item 8 that we will accept monies from suppliers in the following ways to benefit franchisees: (1) as sponsorships for conferences to ensure high-quality programs with reasonable franchisee registration fees; (2) as additional funds to be applied to the NAF; and/or (3) as funds to enable the addition of technology features without adding costs to franchisees. None of these three sources are applied to the revenues or income statement of the franchisor. All three reduce the amounts franchisees would otherwise have to spend on attending conferences, generating marketing leads, and/or implementing new technology features.

Closing Thoughts

In closing, I want to share a few additional FDD decision points for you to consider. We had a couple of terms in our franchise agreement that were included for the right reasons but were administratively burdensome, and I would avoid them in the future.

One example: To encourage franchisees to increase their businesses— a benefit to them and us—we included declining royalty rate schedules above $2 million in annual sales. The challenge lies in realizing when they reach this level and changing the royalty rate accordingly. We hope to fully automate this process in the near future. I don't know that franchisees were necessarily looking for this benefit, and most of our competitors don't include it, so it was probably not a necessary component to our offering.

The second problematic term removed *individual* territory minimum performance requirements under our area development agreement as long as the aggregate revenues of all territories equaled 110 percent of the required individual minimum performance levels. Since territories may have varying successes, I didn't want to penalize owners who showed they could perform in one territory even though another territory fell a little short. With different opening dates of each territory, this has become difficult to administer, and we will remove it from future agreements. (As you will see in chapter 10, our voluntary removal of performance requirements prior to 2010 on second and subsequent territories removed the complexity of this issue. The value to franchisees of the delay in assessing performance requirements was far greater than the benefit of this clause.)

In another variation on the standard agreement, you should look for opportunities to negotiate national contracts for your franchisees to sell their services and/or products. Why? Typically, the sales function is owned by the franchisee, and executing it is her part in following the model. But if I, as the franchisor, am able to negotiate contracts for franchisees, then I should. Yet, because this isn't part of my core function, I want to be able to cover the costs of adding a dedicated position to work on this opportunity. This is a win-win for the franchisor and the franchisee.

BRIGHT IDEA:

We included a higher royalty on national account revenue sources in our FDD (1 percent higher) to offset the cost of the national account leadership position.

• • •

In the next section, we address the concept of leadership and what the focus of the founder/CEO should be over time. We will discuss how, by understanding the keys to leadership, you can build your internal and external teams to support your vision and align employees, franchisees, and suppliers/consultants to enable you to win.

LAYING THE FOUNDATION FOR SUCCESSFUL GROWTH

CHAPTER 3

Defining the Vision, Culture, and Organization to Win

In my opinion, the most successful and reputable franchise systems are the ones in which the founders and/or leaders operated company-owned locations first. They had one successful location and then were able to replicate the model to additional locations. How can you franchise something without understanding how the business works and the types of challenges franchisees can expect to face? But the big question is: how do you know when you are ready to leverage your success? We will expand on the tactical evaluation discussed in section 1 by looking at the type of leadership needed to enable all key stakeholders to see clearly the vision of the future that you are building.

Determining when a business owner is ready to franchise will be unique to each person. Generally, I would advise a minimum of three to five years and an ability to replicate to at least a second company-owned location before considering franchising (or, in certain cases, several additional company-owned locations may be more appropriate). Beyond that, the necessary key steps in franchise expansion are not unique. You need a profitable business model that can be replicated, and you need a market demand for your product or service or the differentiation of your product or service. The great news is that the time you spend improving the profitability of your "pilot" locations and enabling the business to run without a dependency on you *both* improves your success in the pilot *and* prepares you for franchising. When you have done your groundwork, your résumé should show potential franchisees what your experience has taught you and what you can teach them, so that they have the opportunity to replicate your model and achieve success.

In the beginning of structuring a franchise system, there will be natural modifications to adapt to local market nuances. New franchisees will be nervous and will need help in navigating the inevitable challenges. Being able to say from a place of authority, "I did that" or "I experienced that, too," gives you immense credibility. You have walked in the shoes that your franchisees will walk in, and this is the single best education and experience you can have as a franchisor. You are also passionate about your business and the services or goods you provide to customers, and you will be the best one to transfer your passion and enthusiasm to your franchisees.

You will obviously need to learn franchising. You will. You learned your business's industry and succeeded in it. Now you will leverage both the advice in this book and your past success to take your business on a new journey to leverage franchising to grow. Your ability to build teams— to apply leadership—will allow you to succeed in franchising. There are unique skills related to leading a franchise system, and they differ from leading employees: A franchisor must be able to influence others to take action, follow systems, and build teams. Influential leadership requires a specific set of skills that a franchisor must have or develop.

There are multiple facets of leadership. You will roll up your sleeves in the early stage as a franchisor and wear multiple hats. To grow and expand, you will need to transition out of the day-to-day tasks, entrusting them to new employees as you begin to work more *on* the business of franchising, assuring staff in your current business that they can run, grow, and succeed without you.

Transitioning into a New Role

Your first step in franchise leadership is to ensure that your current company-owned business can run without you. Do you have the leadership team in place to run the day-to-day operations and be accountable for delivering on the goals you have for the business? This is critical. Your team must be able to function with less than five hours per month of your leadership, and you must be confident that the team can meet your expectations. Having a self-sufficient team managing the current business so that you can really focus your efforts on the successful launch of your franchise system is the best place to start in your journey to franchising.

The two hardest lessons I learned as I transitioned from running my company-owned operation to being a franchisor are definitely worth sharing.

AVOID THIS PITFALL:

I didn't invest in having a leader oversee the company-owned operations while I focused on my franchisees.

When my franchisees needed me, I focused on them fully, which was the right thing to do, but it also meant that my company-owned operation, which had been my source of positive cash flow, suffered financially when I took my eye off the ball. I would have spent less adding a leader for company-owned operations than I lost in profits from losing focus.

The second lesson is related, in that I did not protect my company-owned employees from having to "do their day job" while also having to support franchisees too.

You have an opportunity to learn from my experiences and prepare your business to maintain its success as you transition to franchising.

Prepare yourself and your existing employees for the transitions that lie ahead by clearly documenting your expectations for each person, including yourself, during the shift.

AVOID THIS PITFALL:

Secure adequate personnel so that you have dedicated resources for the company-owned operations and different resources (including you) focused on franchising.

This transition to franchising also means that you must develop a new set of skills to influence others. Franchisees are not employees, and they are investing rather than being guaranteed a salary. Franchisees must have confidence in your leadership, and they must believe that following the model is the fastest, best path to success. Franchisees will not follow blindly; in becoming franchisees, they are taking a calculated risk that you know what you are doing. Along the way, changes that you introduce must be qualitatively and quantitatively documented and communicated clearly to influence franchisees to follow.

Transitioning from Founder to CEO

As you launch your franchise system, you will be involved in everything, primarily so that you understand each area well enough to know how to hire for the roles as you grow your franchise system. In the beginning, you will support each of your franchisees, and they will naturally not want to stop dealing with you when it is time for you to grow into the CEO role and you begin to add support personnel who will work with them daily. This is your second transition—from founder to CEO.

Early on, you are just trying to survive, giving great support to your franchisees and delaying the costs of the next hire. You will progress to investing in talent to grow once you have the mental and emotional security of getting past 10 franchisees. This will be an adjustment for you to hire and turn over responsibilities to someone else and empower them to deliver the needed results. While this is a transition for you, do not underestimate that it is also a huge transition for the franchisees. They will resist being supported by the newbie rather than by you. It will be critical for you to make time to be visible in group calls or webinars, so they don't feel as though you've abandoned them. I recommend using two-way calls to stay in touch. This could be a monthly call for an hour, which is not a big commitment of time but will have great cultural impact for your franchisees.

You may evolve later in your franchise business life cycle and consider adding a president, for the day-to-day running of the franchise. This type of investment can free you up to promote the brand externally, launch new brands, travel, or work more strategically *on* the business. I began considering adding a president in 2008 (it didn't happen until two years later), as I believed that I would enjoy my role much more—and I would be more valuable to my employees and my franchisees—if I were able to focus on the strategy and the culture and on developing the talent to enable the future growth of our enterprise.

Filling the role of president was a big decision for me, and I benefited from engaging a few advisors to interview candidates for this role because they knew me so well and knew the stamp I had made on BrightStar. I asked my strategic coach, Juli Betwee, and two franchise mentors, Rocco Fiorentino and Geoff Hill, to interview a candidate for me who had years of experience in a senior leadership position with a competitor.

Juli, Rocco, and Geoff each had their own valuable insights, but the collective feedback fell into two key areas: (1) In the two years since meeting the candidate, I had learned and accomplished so much that I was now at the candidate's level, and if I were to invest in this role externally then I should hire someone who could take it to the next level; and (2) my shoes would be easier to fill by developing someone internally who could take on responsibility gradually over time and gain the buy-in and trust of the franchisees and employees. This is some of the best advice I ever received. The key here is that I would not necessarily have come to the same conclusion without involving those I trusted in the process and listening to their input.

The timing was ideal for gathering this insight, as it was received shortly before I hired a former franchisee as the VP of operations. He didn't know my plan (to develop him to take on the role of president) until mid-2010, but I spent all of 2009 and early 2010 transitioning more and more to him, letting him make the decisions and dealing with specific franchisee issues. When I announced his promotion to president at our franchisee conference, there was absolute acceptance. I judge succession planning to be effective when you are able to seamlessly "move" someone into a new, higher role because you had already been slowly moving the responsibilities and developing the skills and assigning the authority prior to the announcement. And the great news about promoting from within is that it creates opportunities in the organization to backfill the position of the recently promoted person.

What Is the Leader's Role?

As you begin planning on growth from 10 franchisees to 50 franchisees and beyond, more time needs to be spent *on* the business. This is when you must begin focusing on the big picture of where the business can go and how you will get it there.

I believe the leader has three primary roles in this regard: (1) Set the vision by applying a strategic planning process and investing for the future; (2) serve as the chief culture officer; and (3) build an organization of talented individuals who are capable of growing with the franchise organization. Let's look at each role more fully.

Set the Vision

Your franchisees and your employees need to have confidence in you as the leader of your business; they need to know that you know where the business is capable of going and how to get there. The larger your business gets, the more time you must spend away from the daily details and on the big picture. Your time must be allocated intentionally to strategic thinking and looking outside the organization for the threats to and opportunities for your business and your industry.

After we had 10 franchisees, I tried to dedicate 10–20 percent of my time on the big picture for our business. Now that we have 175 franchisees, I dedicate about 80 percent of my time to setting the strategy and developing the organization that I need to meet my long-term vision of what our business will be. It took four years to go from 10 percent to 80 percent, but I worked on intentionally building my organization to free my time; that enabled me to focus on the strategic opportunities that could be created.

I use a five-step strategic planning process for the franchisor entity that is facilitated annually by my strategic coach. This is a thorough process that gets the entire organization on the same page, working toward common goals and a shared vision of the future.

In step 1 we assess honestly where we are right now—looking at both the good and the not so good of our business. Step 2 involves an environmental scan, in which we try to look at lots of external information and how the trends may impact our business. The environmental scan includes a thorough evaluation of our business compared to our competitors, think-tank information on where the industry is going, futurist information, and a macro environment review of consumer confidence, access to credit, regulation, etc. We include the franchisees in this step by sending a questionnaire for them to complete to let us know at their local level what the strengths and weaknesses of the model are and what they see as the threats to, and opportunities for, their business and/or our industry. We utilize these inputs to prepare a SWOT (strengths, weaknesses, opportunities, threats) analysis for the brand and then for three different constituencies: franchisees, customers, and franchisor stakeholders including corporate staff. We will add a fourth view for caregivers (field employees) next year to address access to healthcare labor issues.

In step 3 we look at where we want to be at some point in the future (initially, three years out; now we are building the capability to look 10 years out) informed by the environmental scan and recognizing where we are now. During step 4 we define the strategic initiatives that will be needed to get us from our current state to where we want to be in our future state. Step 5 involves defining the projects that are needed and how we will fund them to support the strategies necessary to reach our vision.

Here are some of the critical points of this five-step process that make it very successful:

+ Use an outside facilitator so the entire team can participate
+ Be honest in the assessment of the current state of the business
+ Gather all managers together in an off-site retreat to thoroughly review the information in steps 1, 2, and 3 and prepare a SWOT analysis (this aligns the team in seeing the vision and what it will take to get there)
+ Seek input from franchisees through a survey as to their SWOT analysis of the brand and their local opportunity
+ Involve the managers in identifying and assessing the projects for step 5 so they own the projects and have the successful implementation of projects in their quarterly goals.

The long-term success of the business is related to the level of emphasis on and investment in implementing the strategies needed to move from the current state to the future state. The level of investment that the business is willing to make will determine the number and size of the projects. When we saw that there was no single market leader in our industry, for instance, I made a significant investment of slightly more than 100 percent of our prior year's profit to invest in technology and marketing strategies to capture market share and stake our position as the market leader. It was important to make this investment but also to set the expectation that this level of investment could not be made every year—as the longevity of the franchisor, and hence the brand, requires a strong franchisor balance sheet.

My challenge as a leader of a franchise is prioritizing the strategic initiatives—balancing franchisees' requests with what I know must be done to remain competitive. Our big breakthrough came in 2010 when we involved our Franchise Advisory Council (FAC) in setting the priorities for the projects that we would execute in 2010–2011. As the leader, I knew that three of the projects were critical to ensuring our competitive survival and differentiation, and I set the top three projects and the dollars. I then shared the total amount that we would invest and the estimated cost of each of the projects identified through the SWOT analysis compiled from franchisee and employee input. The FAC then listened to the senior staff pitch each of the projects and the benefits of each. The FAC then weighed in on the order of the fourth, fifth, and sixth projects and confirmed that the total costs of all six projects fell within the financial guidelines of what we could invest.

Having the FAC provide input in the setting of priorities also gave us a strong ability to focus on those agreed-to priorities. We had permission to say no to any requests that conflicted with these priorities. This integrated approach to setting the priorities for the organization aligned all parties collectively to remain focused on the initiatives that would have the greatest impact on the franchise system. Likewise, by having this open communication of what we committed to invest in 2010–2011, we had FAC support to set realistic investment levels for the initiatives selected for 2012 to be more in line with R&D expenditure and investment best practice levels equal to 4 percent of revenues. We used 4 percent of the estimated 2011 franchisor revenues to set the dollar limit of strategic initiatives for 2012 that we will prioritize with input from the FAC.

The five-step vision process dedicates time to strategic planning and to the communication needed to align the organization with a shared set of goals. Employees and franchisees want to follow a leader who knows where the franchise organization is going and how to get it there. Employees and franchisees also want to contribute to help the organization reach its potential. Engaging the team to identify and support the initiatives needed to help the business reach its potential is the key to establishing a high-performing company and franchise system culture.

Serve as the Chief Culture Officer

One of the most important roles a leader has is in establishing the culture of the organization. Often the leader may not know the impact he has on the culture. I like to be intentional about the culture that I want in our organization—both for the employees and for the franchisees.

As discussed, our culture is one of openness. Our franchisees know the sales performance, gross margin, client and employee retention, etc., of one another. This fosters healthy competition but also a willingness to help one another so that all franchisees can improve. We also openly share our goals and our financials with employees.

We are a high-growth organization, so we do work hard and have big goals. We also take time to have fun. We celebrate our wins publicly and work with one another openly to improve when we fail. We treat one another like family. I am known as a hugger, so that affection and affinity for our people is important to me in setting the culture of the organization.

Our focus on helping our franchisees succeed and always striving to improve their unit economics is an intentional message that is known to the organization in all that we do and in the investments we make. We are committed to helping franchisees execute the business model when they are doing the activities required, delivering the highest service and quality to represent the brand well, and investing in the marketing and recruiting required by the business. We are also committed to helping franchisees exit quickly—and for the best possible price—when they are unable to commit the time or resources to executing the model. We do this because we are equally focused on the greater good for the family as a whole and must ensure that our support resources are focused on the franchisees who will make the best use of the resources. We want 80 percent of our resources to be focused on supporting franchisees who are committed to succeeding, rather than following the normal 80/20 rule, whereby 80 percent of the resources are focused on the 20 percent who are not invested in following the model.

Cultures often take on the tone and personality of the leader.

BRIGHT IDEA:

For an optimal culture in a franchise organization, there is one pervasive element that must exist: shared success.

The franchisor cannot succeed without franchisees' being successful and growing. Franchisees cannot succeed without the franchisor's being successful. The franchisor cannot succeed without high-performing employees. Employees cannot succeed without the success of both franchisees and the franchisor, because success means bonus opportunities, growth opportunities, and possibly long-term incentive opportunities. All three constituencies must understand their interdependency in the outcome.

Build the Organization for Growth

I learned the hard way over the past five years that hiring good people to fill an immediate need rather than hiring for what I needed to meet my goals in the following two years was cheaper but was also an inhibitor to growth.

BRIGHT IDEA:

Once I began building job descriptions for the job that I needed two years out, and hired for that, the pieces the organization needed to grow began to fall into place.

To build an organization that is capable of growth, you must recruit talent that fits the culture, and you must also be intentional about how to retain exceptional talent. Let's look at the role of recruiter and talent developer that the leader needs to play.

The Leader's Role as Recruiter

As the leader, you always have to be recruiting. Even if you are not ready to hire for a position, you must spend time thinking about what roles you will need in the next one to two years. Once you know what positions you will need in the future, it is important to place yourself in situations to meet the people you may want to hire. Consider what events these candidates attend and the online groups they are members of. Find a way to spend time among the pool of potential candidates in their circles. I share my vision for the future organization with the members of my team so that they, too, become recruiters of the talent that we need for future growth.

It is also paramount for the leader to be heavily involved in his industry. The leader needs to be visible so that the top talent seeks out opportunities to work for his company. This takes time, but it is a multiplier of your ability to recruit and hire the employees you want and need to grow your business.

The Leader's Role as Talent Developer

While most organizations have a human resources function that plays a role in developing talent and/or ensuring that managers are developing their people, I believe that what the CEO prioritizes and engages in is what actually gets done. If the CEO talks about the importance of developing talent and creating succession plans for key positions, then the organization will make this a priority.

BRIGHT IDEA:

Our breakthrough came with recognizing that leadership was responsible for ensuring that employees were being developed for their future roles and understood the opportunities the future held.

I believe it is critical for employees to know explicitly what their role is today and what their role could become over time. The future state must be defined with clear objective goals so that employees know what their titles and compensation will be, once they reach those goals. It puts the accountability for the outcomes and the development plan of the skills needed to get there with the employee. The employee becomes empowered to reach his potential.

I ensure that our top-performing employees receive an opportunity to attend healthcare or franchise industry and/or role-specific events as well as to attend job-specific training to help them be ready for the next role. Brand-new managers attend "new manager" training, for example. As employees take on more project management responsibility, we train them in that new skill so they can be successful. We make a conscious commitment to an investment in developing our high-potential talent. Their boss will serve as a mentor and is expected to help guide them up the career ladder. I personally am involved in reviewing and providing feedback on the development plans of the top 20 percent of our employees.

Ultimately, as the organization grows, the leader needs to get out of the middle and have the organization progress on its own. When I began including the broader organization in the annual strategic planning exercise and the priorities for the organization, I got out of the middle because the organization knew collectively where we were, where we were going, and what needed to be done to get there. I didn't have to call all the plays to get incremental results; the team had the whole playbook and could run them totally on their own. Setting the vision for the organization and doing so as a group allows everyone to be driving to the same goals; no one is waiting around for the boss to tell her what to do next. The path has been set and the team has been empowered to deliver the needed results.

Especially for Founders

I wanted to include a special section for those of you who are founders, who have built your business and who will build your franchise system. As you embark on building a much larger organization, I want to challenge you to think about the following questions to help you get the most from the journey:

1. What role(s) do you most enjoy?
2. Are you a business builder (strategy/sales) or a business maintainer (operations/finance)?
3. Do you enjoy being the external face and voice of the business?

4. Do you want to continue to run the day-to-day operations of your larger business?

The reason I think it is important to ask these questions is that, as your business grows, you, as the founder, have more opportunity to choose the role you enjoy the most. Think about Bill Gates not wanting to be CEO and instead positioning himself as chief software architect (and then subsequently chief philanthropist, through the Bill and Melinda Gates Foundation). You will have the same opportunities to decide what role you like best or whether you want to stay involved full-time in the day-to-day business at all.

By understanding the answers to the four questions above, you will know better who to hire to fill the holes of the organization that result from your choice not to do certain functions. You will also be able to identify talent internally that you can develop to fill future roles to allow you to transition to the role you love. By knowing how long you want to be involved day-to-day and what role you want within the organization, you can start with the end in mind when you begin designing your future organization—much as I did in hiring and developing my vice president of operations for the role of BrightStar Care president.

For me, BrightStar is my passion, and I can't imagine not being active in my business daily. I did realize, however, that I enjoy building much more than maintaining. This realization created an opportunity for me to move up as the CEO by investing and grooming an internal candidate to take over as the brand president. I will likewise invest in brand presidents for each of the new brands I start. While I thought my background as a CPA would have aligned more with being in the maintenance of the day-to-day operations of the business, I have found that my love is for strategy development, people development, and shaping company culture.

As important as it is to focus on what you need to intentionally focus on, it is equally important to be aware of and acknowledge the potential traps that founders can find themselves in, such as the following: being afraid to let go, hiring friends and/or family who can't meet the growing demands of the position, the tendency to push information down to franchisees without pulling information up, and being afraid to hire employees better than themselves or to intentionally hire "yes" people.

Closing Thoughts

If you do decide to transition some or all of the functions to someone else, prepare for the transition. Even though you are executing a plan you designed, you want to avoid ending up on a short-term emotional roller coaster. That's where I found myself as I turned over some of my responsibilities to my brand president. It was natural, in hindsight, but I wish I had planned for the impact. BrightStar is like my firstborn, and transitioning some of the day-to-day business and some of the visibility with my franchisees was difficult. It was ultimately the best decision for me, for the future of the organization, and for our franchisees. My best contribution is in setting the vision. I now am able to spend 80 percent of my time looking at best practices and trends outside of our organization and bringing them back to be implemented to help us achieve our potential.

· · ·

To support your franchisees, you will need to assemble a great team. Plan for and seek great talent so that you can always meet your franchisees' needs. Turn the page for the most critical component to the success of great companies—the internal team.

CHAPTER 4

Creating a Great Team to Help You Grow

Great teams are necessary to build and sustain great companies. Average teams will never build or sustain great companies—only average companies or failing companies. It really is true that there is no "I" in "team." I once rolled my eyes at that saying, too, but as I've reflected on our success, I've realized the truth of that statement.

I think it is equally important to think about how you define your team. Is it limited to your staff? Does it include your franchisees? What about your advisors, suppliers, and consultants? For me, a team includes all of these. In chapter 10, you will learn how to build an intentional culture so that franchisees are naturally a part of the team. And in chapter 5 we will discuss how suppliers and consultants, as well as a board of advisors, work to build a much stronger and effective team.

This chapter reveals a lot of our secrets to building a great team in any industry, from senior leadership throughout the entire organization, whether it is franchised or not. Though some of the tips on potential structures and ratios may be applicable only to franchising, the overall content about building a high-performance culture should be appropriate and, I hope, valuable to all companies.

Building a team begins with identifying and selecting talent. I will share some broad thoughts on building teams from a general perspective and then walk through a second section that focuses on building the right team specific to your infrastructure evolution as your franchise system grows. The final section is about linking pay to performance, which is a critical component in attracting, developing, motivating, and retaining great talent. Selecting people who are passionate and committed to our higher mission—of providing care to families and enabling individuals to own businesses and create jobs—and then aligning their compensation and recognition around accomplishing a set of individual and *shared* goals allows everyone in the organization to be fully engaged. The team knows where we are going and what their contribution will be individually and as part of their department or as part of a project team to get us there. We all share core values of positive attitude, passion, and commitment: We work hard, we play hard, we have fun, and we move forward *together*.

Identifying and Selecting Talent

You should always be networking for talent. As mentioned in the previous chapter, you will always need great people, so embracing the role of recruiter is an important and key role for the CEO/founder. Finding great talent comes from using multiple sources: networking, search firms (paid recruiters), and job boards. I prefer to leverage networking for positions that I have directly managed before. When I am adding a position to my organization that I have not managed previously, I will consider using a search firm to help me evaluate what I am seeking in the position and what to expect, and to serve as a conduit during the on-boarding process.

There are two types of recruiting searches: retained searches and non-retained ones. For the very high-level positions where you are likely sourcing someone who is not even looking for a job or you are performing a confidential search, you may consider a retained search whereby you pay some portion upfront and the recruiter seeks the right person to fill the job, exclusively for you. On the other hand, a non-retained search can be placed with one or multiple firms, and you pay only when you hire a candidate they have presented to you.

One of my best-ever hires, my chief of staff, came through a search firm under a retained search agreement, and though I hate paying headhunter fees as much as anyone else, in this case the ROI was priceless. I have used job boards like Career Builder and have also networked among good people. Other successful hires have come through employee recommendations and by bringing franchisees in to join the corporate team.

Proactive Networking for Talent

Networking for the positions that you know you will need in the next 12 to 18 months can be a proactive strategy to allow ample time to find great people to fill jobs just at the time you will need them. Bear in mind, however, that there is a difference between getting a name or referral from someone and getting a recommendation. In the past I have asked people in my network if they knew anyone who would be appropriate for a job opening at BrightStar Care. It was great to get leads, but I made the mistake of interviewing more lightly and not checking references as I normally would.

AVOID THIS PITFALL:
It's paramount—no matter what business you're in—to avoid treating the name you receive from someone you trust as though it were a recommendation.

All candidates must follow the same interview process and reference checks to protect the integrity of the company you're trying to build.

On the other hand, I have had tremendous success when existing employees recommend people they know for open positions. I can think of no higher compliment than an employee suggesting to someone he knows and respects to join our company.

Attitude Is Everything

I hire attitude first because skills can be taught or improved if the right attitude is there. Every time I have deviated from this—yes, *every* single time—I have been burned, whether I was "sold" by a great salesperson in an interview or fell for a résumé. In my experience, if someone has never succeeded as part of a fast-paced team, hasn't thrived in or been a part of a highly accountable organization, hasn't gone above and beyond to reach goals, or hasn't been a part of a company growing by triple digits, that person probably won't magically start performing on all cylinders once hired onto the team.

True motivation and a positive attitude are internally generated. I may like to think of myself as a high-energy leader who inspires others, but the reality is that I won't be able to inspire anyone to take an action she is not willing to take otherwise. Those who are willing to work hard to meet a deadline, to take a client call at night or over the weekend, to drive performance, and to respond to the CEO's e-mail after hours will take your inspiration and run through brick walls. Those who do the minimum work required in order to keep a job, but no more, won't suddenly start giving more because of your high energy, the high-growth atmosphere, or their peers. Use behavioral interviewing techniques to ensure that prospective employees can demonstrate experience in a fast-paced organization or to show where they have proactively improved a process or led a project. For example, I want to hear about actual experiences from those in field support, so I ask them to tell me about (1) their most struggling franchisee and what actions they took and what was the result; (2) their best-performing franchisee and how they specifically supported him; and

(3) their franchisee with the worst attitude and what actions they took and what the result was. I am looking for different approaches because franchisees are individuals and need customized support; I am also looking for their ability to initiate and manage difficult conversations.

Building the Right Team

The ideal team is not built overnight and it will not be built flawlessly. You will add people to the team who may not adapt to the environment or may not be able to develop quickly enough to keep pace with what you will need as the business grows. That said, there are a few tips that can improve your odds for hiring talent for the long haul that fit your culture and what you need as the organization evolves.

Always think about what background or skills are critical to a position. For example, if the majority of your sales growth comes through franchise brokers (brokers are external resources that prequalify and introduce prospective franchisees to you; we will discuss this further in chapter 7), it would be important to hire franchise salespeople and team leaders with existing relationships and past success with brokers. Likewise, if your franchisee's success is based on sales efforts at a local level, it would be important to hire field support people who have experience and are successful at it. It is obviously unrealistic to think that someone with no sales experience who is hired for field support will be able to grow sales.

Do not limit hiring to candidates with franchising experience. In the shared services areas such as marketing, finance, human resources, and technology, find the best employees in terms of their skill set, experience, and attitude, regardless of their knowledge of franchising. All of our senior management team and any other of our "Top 10," which we will discuss later in this chapter, are required to be International Franchise Association Certified Franchise Executives (CFEs), and if they are not CFEs when they are hired, they are enrolled in the program and attend the annual IFA convention to raise their level of knowledge about franchising—for themselves and our team. However, in the areas of field support and franchise sales, I do try hard to recruit from within the franchise industry because these are highly nuanced positions, critical to growth and to the success of our franchise.

My addition of a franchisee to the corporate team worked so well the first time in October 2008 that I did it again in early 2010. Franchisees know what is required to run a successful operation within your system, and they will help improve your model for other franchisees, which is critical to long-term success. I recommend ensuring that the franchisee had profit-and-loss accountability in her corporate life before becoming a franchisee and can demonstrate that she understands that both the franchisee and the franchisor must win financially. You need someone in corporate to have the franchisee perspective, but you also need to ensure that she will focus on improving the system and the franchisor's results too.

My first franchisee to be hired onto the corporate team was seamlessly promoted to president within two years of his hire, during which time I let him make more and more decisions and deal with specific franchisee issues. This individual had large department and business unit profit-and-loss accountability for billion-dollar divisions and/or companies in his corporate life, and I spent time with him to be assured that he could represent franchisee and franchisor interests. I identified another franchisee with strong prior technology background who I felt could also represent the franchisees in what the technology could do and in the scalability and controllability of costs that I needed as the franchisor. Our senior VP of technology—who had been a franchisee for over three years—accepted my offer after seeing the large investment I was willing to make in technology and my commitment to using technology as a major differentiator and method of achieving scalability and excellence. (At this writing we are in the middle of a 12-month technology upgrade costing over $1.8 million.) Our focus on technology provides our brands with the tools and innovation to stay ahead of our competition because we are not limited by a third party's willingness to upgrade its software.

It is hard to entice franchisees who are performing well (and of course those are the ones you want to hire) to leave working for themselves to return to the corporate world. We have been fortunate that our franchisees are passionate about our brand and are looking for ways they can have the greatest positive impact. Some also enjoy an opportunity to assume a role that utilizes their deep knowledge and experience in a functional area, like technology or operations, rather than having to apply the broad array of skills needed as a business owner.

Evolving the Infrastructure

You may have a small number of people in the beginning, but hiring will need to ramp up as your system grows. It is more important and relevant to consider the number of employees needed to handle the number of franchisees than to think about the changes that will need to be made in infrastructure over time. Our philosophy was to hire in advance of growth, and that is why our ratio of employee to franchisee was low in years one through five. This strategy of hiring in advance worked for us because we were able to see others in our industry consistently adding franchisees each year and we were confident that we would grow into our larger-than-necessary personnel structure. Your industry segment and its growth history and capitalization will determine the level of infrastructure you can invest in and how early. The evolution of our corporate infrastructure, shown year by year later in this chapter, will assist you in considerations of what positions to hire and which to outsource, and when these positions should be evaluated.

Scale in infrastructure in terms of productivity, measured through revenue per dollar of payroll, begins to normalize and reach top quartile performance in the industry in years six and thereafter. This shows that while we have one of the lowest employee-to-franchisee ratios, and hence high payroll investments, the support staff are driving revenue high enough to justify the investment.

One lesson I learned very early on was to make sure the position title matched the job description.

AVOID THIS PITFALL:
I initially brought people in and gave them titles that were too high and did not really reflect their authority and ability to act independently.

People love titles, so it is an easy and inexpensive thing to give, but knowing that the company will grow will make it a challenge later. I would recommend hiring individuals laterally with the same title as previously held and then performing a compensation and title review after six months.

I had to go through several conversations in 2008 and 2009 to reset titles to appropriate levels so we could fill in the organization more accurately. A vice president's role in an organization that had reached system-wide sales of $100 million annually was quite different from what the role was when the organization was at $10 million. This may be obvious, but it is never easy to discuss with an employee. I would rather bring people in at lower levels and give them every opportunity to progress and take on more responsibility and earn titles that accurately reflect their responsibilities as the enterprise grows. This is the approach I began taking in late 2008, and it has served me well.

Another lesson I learned early on is that those who start with you may not stay with you. You may have employees who cannot keep up with the pace of change, who may not take the initiative to improve their skills so that the company's growth is an opportunity for them rather than a threat, or who have poor attitudes. I have found that having direct conversations as early as possible and documenting the gaps that the employee must address thoroughly lays the groundwork to improve performance to acceptable levels or to ensure the proper documentation for a clean termination. You may have some employees who are less comfortable with ever-changing technology, even though nearly all aspects of business are enhanced by or dependent on it, and as you implement new tools they will resist them. Often these are the very employees who will be positioned to train, reinforce, and influence use of these technology tools by the franchisees. You should make training available to them, but if they are not embracing it after several opportunities, you need to part ways.

After going through a few painful situations in which great people were no longer able to meet the needs of our larger organization, I changed my hiring approach. Things dramatically improved when I decided to hire people whose skills exceeded what we needed. I recognized that if I was willing to make the higher compensation investment, this higher talent could be a part of the recipe to actually get us to the revenue level we wanted to be at two or three years later—faster, too, quite likely.

The Early Years

In this section, I walk through the evolution of our organization by calendar year. I have provided the number of franchisees at the beginning and at the end of each year to illustrate support ratios. My intention in showing you specifically how our organization grew over time is to share the order in which we hired certain positions and to show whether there were alternatives we would have considered if we had known about them. I will highlight the additions but will not specifically address title changes, as some titles needed to be adjusted down (as mentioned earlier) and some were adjusted up according to employees' ability to grow their skills to take on more responsibility as we grew. I also have excluded all personnel dedicated to company-owned operations from the discussion and from the organizational charts.

At the conclusion of each year there is a chart that visually depicts our historical organizational, with a recap to help you process the information. This will help you understand the order of positions and how your assumptions for your financial statements will change based upon whether you maintain your own technology platform or not. Most companies will not invest in technology the way BrightStar has (that is, license the technology to our franchisees). The summaries therefore highlight the personnel in the technology area, and the revenues and earnings per employee excluding both the investments in technology and the revenues derived from technology. As of 2010, we moved our technology into a separate entity to allow better comparisons to the majority of franchisors who have not built their own proprietary technology and invested to license it to their franchisees.

From the information in the following section, you will also be able to consider your strengths and how they influence decisions to delay hiring for some positions, as you'll learn was the case with our finance hire (in hindsight). To assist with demonstrating the level of investment and how it impacted revenues and EBITDA per employee, I will disclose these metrics for each of the years, with technology revenue and profits as well as employee count excluded, and the breakdown of our employees into three key areas—franchisee support, technology, and administration. Franchisee support includes BrightStart, field support, preopening support, national accounts, the support center, and franchisee operations. Administration includes franchise sales, marketing, finance, human resources, executive, and learning and development (training).

With that, let's walk through how we built our team and provide you a vision for building your team.

2005

I began and ended the year with no open franchisees, but I sold one franchise before the end of the year.

The additions and/or changes for the year included the following.

FRANCHISEE SUPPORT ADDITIONS/CHANGES:

I hired a person who would be responsible for supporting franchisees and assisting with training—this was a seasoned person from my industry and from franchising. The addition of this seasoned field support professional (vice president of sales training and field support) was a huge help. It may seem early to have hired this position before we opened a franchise, but I felt that I would need to work with this person for a couple of months to get him up to speed on our business model, our vision, and our values. I also knew that I would be training new franchisees and that I would need help training the sales areas.

TECHNOLOGY ADDITIONS/CHANGES:

In early 2005 I hired an IT director to support our technology platform and work with our external programmers until we could build an internal technology team.

ADMINISTRATION ADDITIONS AND/OR CHANGES:

I added two positions during the year. The first was a controller to relieve me of some of the accounting functions so that I could focus more on the new responsibilities that being a franchisor required. I also brought in someone who had no franchising experience to handle franchise sales. I thought I would be able to train this person to handle franchise sales, but within six months, I knew she was not the right person for the job. Fortunately, my co-founder and husband, J.D., rescued me by taking over this role.

Both of my administration hires were a mistake. In hindsight, I would never have hired someone to handle franchise sales. I now believe that the founder should interact with the prospects when selling the first 10 to 25 units. They are taking a huge leap of faith that the franchisor will really get to 50, to 100 and beyond, and they need to know whom they are buying into. At the earliest stages, prospects are buying the leaders as much as the brand, concept, and industry, maybe more. Before the end of the year, I rectified my mistake and replaced the employee with J.D.

I also would not have hired a controller that early. Hire entry-level finance talent. This is not just because I am a CPA, but more because of what is truly required in that department at this stage. Outside CPAs can be brought in a few hours a month to supplement the entry-level talent at a much lower combined cost.

AVOID THIS PITFALL:

If I could do it again, I would hire a strong assistant or an accounting clerk who could handle of lot of the repetitive tasks, copying, etc., so my time could be freed up to handle the new responsibilities of being a franchisor.

I recommend that founders keep high-level (high-salary) functions that they have solid experience with as long as possible and add administrative bandwidth (at lower salary levels) as needed to support the founders.

SUMMARY:

I had five employees, including J.D. and me, supporting the launch at the end of 2005. We had sold one franchise and would open it in March 2006. There were negligible revenues in 2005, so key metrics are excluded below.

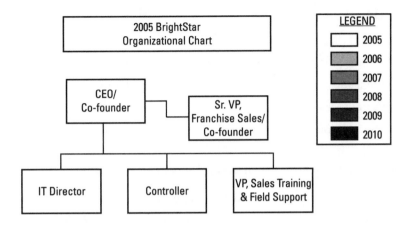

2005 RECAP:

Open Locations:

+ 0 (1 sale had been made but it would not open until 2006)

Staff Hired:

+ 4 – 1 replaced with co-founder (net of 3 additional employees in 2005)

Functions Outsourced:

+ Legal is fully outsourced. Expected partially in house 2012.
+ IT development partially outsourced. Fully in house by the end of 2007.

End-of-Year Organization by Category:

+ Franchisee Support: 1
+ Technology: 1
+ Administration: 3

2006

We began 2006 with no locations open and by the end of the year had opened 10 locations (as well as sold three more locations that were not open as of year's end).

The additions and/or changes for the year included the following.

FRANCHISEE SUPPORT ADDITIONS/CHANGES:

We added a position dedicated to supporting franchisees with state licensure and regulations and in training the franchisees' directors of nursing. We recognized that, since we were not targeting franchisees with a healthcare background, we needed someone as part of the corporate team to assist franchisees in hiring and on-boarding their director of nursing.

ADMINISTRATION ADDITIONS AND/OR CHANGES:

We added a part-time accounting clerk/administrative assistant. Understand what you do well, as dollars are precious. As a CPA, it took me more time to train and manage someone than it took to do the job myself. That wasn't good long term, so adding a part-time accounting clerk to support accounts payable and administrative tasks that support the finance area was a more cost-effective approach. At this stage one strong full-time entry-level accountant would have been enough for our organization leveraging my background as a CPA; I would estimate that using an outside CPA 5 to 10 hours per week in addition to a full-time entry-level accountant would be sufficient to support the finance function for a founder without a strong finance background.

SUMMARY:

At the end of the year we had seven employees, including J.D. and me, supporting 10 open franchisees. This was an extremely high level of support, but I anticipated that in the next year we would sell at least another 25 locations and more than double. I wanted to have the infrastructure in place before the next phase of rapid growth so that new employees had time to learn our business model and culture and support franchisees through that period.

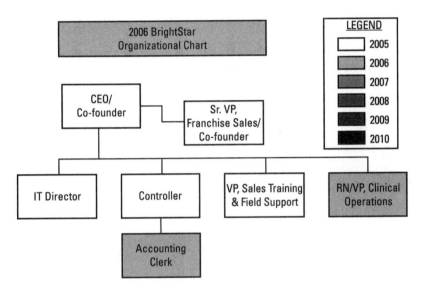

2006 RECAP:

Open Locations (number of locations and franchisees the same):

+ 10

Staff Hired:

+ 2 (total staff: 7)

Functions Outsourced:

+ Legal is fully outsourced. Expected partially in house 2012.
+ IT development partially outsourced. Fully in house by the end of 2007.

End-of-Year Organization by Category:

+ Franchisee Support: 2
+ Technology: 1
+ Administration: 4

2006 Key Metrics:

+ Revenue per $ of payroll: $2.08
+ Revenue per employee: $137,503
+ EBITDA per employee: ($49,129) loss
+ EBITDA as % of revenues: N/A

2007

We began 2007 with 10 locations open and by the end of the year we had 27 locations open. We ended the same year with 47 locations sold, selling 34 locations during the year.

The additions and/or changes for the year included the following.

FRANCHISEE SUPPORT ADDITIONS/CHANGES:

We added a preopening support position that I refer to as a "preopening concierge." The addition of the preopening concierge has been one of my best hires—his positive, service-oriented attitude is unparalleled and sets the top example for the rest of us, as he is a good example of an A-player that many throughout the organization labeled as a "Top 10" (which we will discuss later in this chapter). Our preopening concierge has been critical to getting our franchisees up and functioning as quickly as possible.

TECHNOLOGY ADDITIONS/CHANGES:

We expanded our technology department with the addition of an IT (junior) developer. In 2007, we began building our internal technology team and stopped depending on outside developers to enhance software.

ADMINISTRATION ADDITIONS AND/OR CHANGES:

During the year, we added a franchise sales professional to take over the majority of franchise sales. The franchise sales professional has been one of our best performers for four years. We recognized that, as we were getting a solid base of franchisees, J.D. did not have to remain involved in the sales process for every franchisee. The addition of the franchise sales professional freed up more of J.D.'s time to work on sales strategies and what would be a major rebranding initiative in 2008. Freeing up J.D.'s capacity when we did was important. When you start to recognize that momentum is building, assess your talent bench and contrast that with what you (and your partner, if you have one) offer to ensure you're ready for growth.

SUMMARY:

At the end of the year we had 10 employees, including J.D. and me, supporting 27 open franchisees.

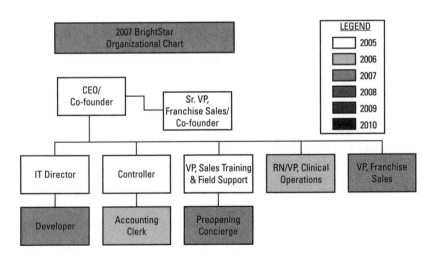

2007 RECAP:

Open Locations (number of locations and franchisees the same):

+ 27

Staff Hired:

+ 3 (total staff: 10)

Functions Outsourced:

+ Legal is fully outsourced. Expected partially in house 2012.
+ By the end of the year, IT development was no longer outsourced.

End-of-Year Organization by Category:

+ Franchisee Support: 3
+ Technology: 2
+ Administration: 5

2007 Key Metrics:

+ Revenue per $ of payroll: $4.37 (our high point before investing heavily in 2008 and 2009 to support our franchisees and enable multi-brands later)
+ Revenue per employee: $310,429
+ EBITDA per employee: $61,481
+ EBITDA as % of revenues: 20%

2008

We began 2008 with 27 locations open and by the end of the year we had 79 locations open. We ended the same year with 105 locations sold, selling 58 locations during the year.

This was a very high-growth year in terms of the number of franchisees added and opened, as well as for building infrastructure. We began 2008 with 10 employees and we finished the year with 27 employees, more than doubling our employee count in a single year.

We made some very key additions in 2008 that I realize in retrospect were critical to our future scalability and the ability for us to move into multiple brands in 2012.

The additions and/or changes for the year included the following.

FRANCHISEE SUPPORT ADDITIONS/CHANGES:

We added a vice president of operations (now the president of BrightStar Care). With many new franchisees, having someone dedicated to operational efficiency and scaling our business effectively was required. Hiring at the vice president level was paramount.

We also added an experienced field support leader as the vice president of field support. This very valuable employee now leads our BrightStart team as vice president and is another one of our highly recognized team members who multiple members of the senior leadership team selected as a "Top 10." In addition, we added four regional field support directors during the year. The additions in field support were more than we needed, but we felt confident that we would continue to grow rapidly in the future, and we wanted our field support team up to speed and working cohesively as a group. We added the four of them between mid-August and the first of December.

In addition, we created a position for the first time dedicated to securing and supporting national accounts. This position was upgraded to a director in 2011.

In summary, in this single year we more than tripled franchisee support resources—growing from three to 10 employees.

TECHNOLOGY ADDITIONS/CHANGES:

We added four additional IT developers, taking our technology team up to six members. I recommend, if you are building proprietary technology, that you make time for frequent reviews of how resources are being applied and if there are any gaps to reach the timeline and quality requirements. Skill gaps within the team take a bit of time to identify, and you will be unable to do that without spending time on a recurring basis. Routinely check the temperature of your team to ensure there aren't "blips" on the horizon that will push you off track. In chapter 5, we will discuss using outside consultants in technology to assist nontechnical CEOs with overseeing and holding accountable this function.

In summary, in this single year we tripled our internal technology resources—growing from two to six employees.

ADMINISTRATION ADDITIONS AND/OR CHANGES:

We began to build our marketing team with the addition of a dedicated marketing and communications coordinator. This position should have been added a lot earlier; we also should have added a marketing leader much earlier, too—a vice president over marketing was finally added in late 2009. The good news is that when we hired our coordinator, we hired really well and this individual was promoted to manager in early 2011. Without a dedicated leader in house, we outsourced projects and the overall project cost was more because of not having someone internally with the bandwidth and experience to manage the projects under way, including the development of collateral materials, the launch of a rebranding effort, and the redesign of a consumer-centric website and social media strategy.

If considering any type of rebranding (which is common for young companies as you evolve your brand and adapt to what your market needs and wants or possibly even demands), even when using an outside branding firm, you should have a dedicated resource in house. Coordination, launch, and implementation are time-consuming activities, and there is a high level of need for someone internally to ensure all implications are considered and the rebranding is done right. Marketing leadership should be added as soon as fiscally possible (likely as soon as you reach 30 to 40 franchisees); regrettably, we waited one to two years longer than we should have in filling that role full-time based upon delaying national ad fund contributions until after 25 locations were opened, as discussed in chapter 2.

Brand development will stave off competition and can help you achieve goals—both on the franchise sales side and in the development of programs that allow your franchisees to be successful in a competitive environment. The level of funding that you will do in advance of collecting national ad fund (NAF) fees should be planned for and proper expectations should be set with franchisees; as the system grows, there will be more NAF dollars to drive visibility and customer awareness, but in the early days you will need to balance what you collect from franchisees with what you know you need to spend; often the timing of these dollars will be out of balance early on. We found it much more economical, and more beneficial to our franchisees, to hire dedicated marketing staff and charge those hires to the NAF, as explained in Item 11 of the FDD, rather than spending much higher amounts with outsourced advertising agencies. We continued to build a team to bring most marketing activities in house.

We also expanded in many other areas, including within the executive offices, in finance and in franchise sales. We added my chief of staff (the answer to a lot of prayers) who was unanimously selected as a "Top 10" by all of the senior team. This addition made me more effective because I had someone to anticipate my needs and act as a strong presence in my absence or on my behalf, allowing me to focus on the matters at hand.

We added an accountant role to our finance team to create capacity for benchmarking and analysis and supporting franchisees.

We significantly expanded our franchise sales area with the addition of another salesperson brought in as a director, as well as adding a manager of contract administration (since promoted to a director) and a franchise sales coordinator (since promoted to a manager). Contract administration during a period of high growth takes a lot of time. This is a critical area for the business and a position that interacts extensively with franchisees, so find someone diligent, brilliant, and ethical who is also a strong, tactful communicator. You'll reap the rewards of that every day. Given the large growth in the franchise sales area and J.D.'s lack of bandwidth and experience in managing personnel, we engaged an outside consultant to help manage the department and build the processes for J.D. to take on that role.

In this single year we more than doubled the administrative foundation—growing from five to 11 employees.

SUMMARY:

At the end of the year we had 27 employees, including J.D. and me, supporting 65 open franchisees.

2008 RECAP:

Open Locations:

+ 79

Open Franchisees:

+ 65

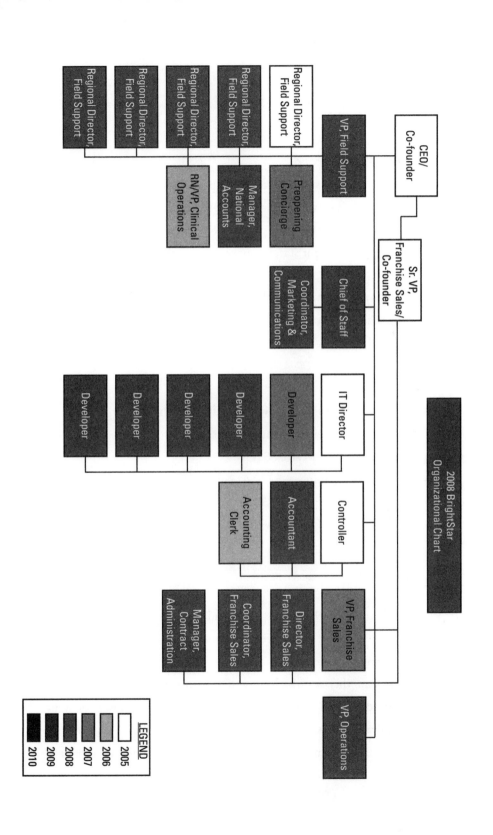

2008 BrightStar Organizational Chart

CEO/Co-founder

Sr. VP, Franchise Sales/Co-founder

VP, Field Support

Regional Director, Field Support

Preopening Concierge

Manager, National Accounts

RN/VP, Clinical Operations

Chief of Staff

Coordinator, Marketing & Communications

IT Director

Developer

Controller

Accountant

Accounting Clerk

VP, Franchise Sales

Director, Franchise Sales

Coordinator, Franchise Sales

Manager, Contract Administration

VP, Operations

LEGEND
2010
2009
2008
2007
2006
2005

Staff Hired:

+ 17 (total staff: 27)

Functions Outsourced:

+ Legal is fully outsourced. Expected partially in house 2012.
+ Branding and strategic marketing. Brought in house late 2009.
+ Franchise sales leadership partially outsourced. All sales personnel employees of BrightStar. In house prior to the end of 2009.

End-of-Year Organization by Category:

+ Franchisee Support: 10
+ Technology: 6
+ Administration: 11

2008 Key Metrics (all lowered due to heavy investment nearly tripling employee count):

+ Revenue per $ of payroll: $2.30
+ Revenue per employee: $320,417
+ EBITDA per employee: $32,580
+ EBITDA as % of revenues: 10%

2009

We began 2009 with 79 locations open, and by the end of the year we had 140 locations open. We also ended the year with 171 locations sold, selling 66 units during the year.

This was another very high-growth year in terms of the number of franchisees added and opened as well as the continued investment in building infrastructure. This second high-growth phase required an increased focus on franchisee support. At the same time, the economy was still sputtering and we felt that continuing to invest in support would allow us to partner with our franchisees through the toughest economic climate we had seen in our lifetime and strengthen our franchisor–franchisee relationships and our system. Remember, we began 2009 with 27 employees after nearly tripling the number of employees in 2008. We ended 2009 with 45 employees, after nearly doubling again the employee count.

The focus in 2009 was to make additions of personnel to reduce each manager's span of control and to begin to have specialists rather than generalists. Having these conversations proactively with employees helped ensure a positive culture; we wanted to demonstrate our willingness to invest in additional resources to enable our employees to be successful and to prevent burnout. All of us recognized that it was natural in the early stages of an organization for nearly every employee and manager to wear multiple hats. As the organization grew, to reach optimal productivity and employee development and retention, the organization had to be sufficiently staffed so that employees could begin to specialize in a functional area rather than being spread thin across multiple areas. This was easier at lower levels within the organization but was the goal at every level. We also knew we had to reduce managers' span of control to increase their bandwidth to develop their employees.

We have plans in place to get each senior leader responsible for only one key area by filling in their organizations in 2011, and by hiring additional C-level executives, including a chief operating officer and chief counsel, in 2012–2013 to add capacity as we launch additional franchise brands. Beginning in 2009, we began to think about and build organizational charts and strategic plans looking five years out, so that we could anticipate the investments that would need to be made to reach our goals and plan for how to develop talent internally to grow with us.

The additions and/or changes for the year included the following.

Franchisee Support Additions/Changes:

We added a manager and two specialists during the year to enable the launch of our support center (we will discuss the support center more fully in chapter 9). We identified that having dedicated support help available for franchisees and their internal team for any need—finding a marketing flyer, using the technology systems, obtaining vendor information, etc.—allowed the franchisees to call one number for anything related to how to find a resource or how to click a button, and then to contact their higher-cost field support director for business reviews, strategies, and skill development. The support center was also necessary to assist our franchisees with adoption of new technology and systems. We have an intense focus on innovation, and the adoption of new programs and tools by franchisees is critical to achieve the ROI on the initiatives.

We restructured field support during the year, creating two separate teams—BrightStart and field support—to provide resources to franchisees with different skill sets based upon their needs to grow sales or operational and leadership needs (we will discuss the strategy behind and implementation of the BrightStart team and the split of support resources into three teams—BrightStart, the support center, and field support—in chapter 9). We hired an additional regional field support director during the year (to replace the one who moved to the new BrightStart team). We also added a BrightStart sales specialist to split preopening responsibilities into operations and sales activities. This role is responsible for the sales activities in the preopening stage as well as supporting the sales effort in the franchisees' first four months.

We also created a new position in response to the difficulty for our franchisees in accessing capital. We added a new position—franchisee finance services director—to assist franchisees with reviewing cash flow and breakeven and with accessing capital. This employee was promoted to a vice president in 2010 and is most definitely a "Top 10" in our organization based on his performance and ongoing contributions.

Lastly, in 2009, we added a director of international operations. This employee resides in Canada, where our first two master franchisees opened in 2011. We invested in a dedicated role so that the resources supporting our domestic franchisees were not strained, and also to dedicate time to understanding the international markets and to ensure that we had a strong investment in supporting our international masters with someone who had experience in homecare in Canada, Australia, and the UK.

TECHNOLOGY ADDITIONS/CHANGES:

We added a quality assurance analyst to our technology department, bringing the team up to seven people.

ADMINISTRATION ADDITIONS AND/OR CHANGES:

We added a vice president of marketing and franchisee on-boarding, a director of marketing, and a second marketing and communications coordinator (separating the roles so that one would be focused on print and the other on search engine optimization and search engine marketing). With the rebranding initiative under way, it was time to make a bigger investment in our marketing team. Again, we had people wearing multiple hats, and this was the year to narrow each employee's focus. By adding three positions, which included a leadership role, we were able to provide more support, initiate competitive marketing programs, and start tracking and setting goals around key metrics of brand awareness.

We added a full-time dedicated trainer as the manager of learning and development.

We added a senior vice president of global sales. (In late 2010 we would have J.D. once again assume leadership over domestic franchise sales and have the president of BrightStar Care assume national accounts, using the dollars to invest in 2011 into incremental positions for international sales and national accounts.)

We recrafted some roles within our finance team, which already had a controller, an accountant, and an accounting clerk. As we started to see the need for more detailed analysis, we promoted our accountant to financial analyst. We backfilled an accountant role that would also support franchisees in the use of the accounting software used system wide.

We also added another franchise sales director (salesperson).

We added our first dedicated human resources position, a human resources manager, as well as some key administrative help to support the rest of the organization, including a paralegal and an administrative assistant.

Summary:

The large investments in marketing and the support center, and the investment to launch the BrightStart program, dramatically improved our ability to support our franchisees.

In summary, at the end of the year we had 45 employees, including J.D. and me, supporting 114 open franchisees. One of these employees was dedicated to international expansion efforts.

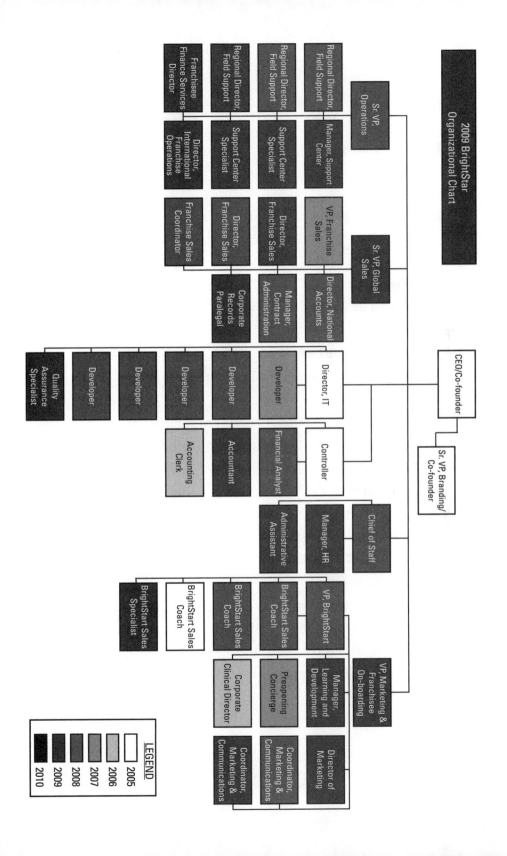

2009 BrightStar Organizational Chart

LEGEND
- 2010
- 2009
- 2008
- 2007
- 2006
- 2005

2009 RECAP:

Open Locations:

+ 140

Open Franchisees:

+ 114

Staff Hired:

+ 18 (total staff: 45)

Functions Outsourced:

+ Legal is fully outsourced. Expected partially in house 2012.

End-of-Year Organization by Category:

+ Franchisee Support: 17 (16 domestic and 1 international)
+ Technology: 7
+ Administration: 21

2009 Key Metrics (significant cont'd investment—positive impact starts 2010):*

+ Revenue per $ of payroll: $2.11
+ Revenue per employee: $217,920
+ EBITDA per employee: $25,009
+ EBITDA as % of revenues: 11%

*Costs for director, international operations, and revenues from international expansion excluded.

2010

We began 2010 with 140 locations open, and by the end of the year we had 198 locations open. We began the year with 171 locations sold and ended it with 244 locations sold.

In 2010, we dramatically expanded our technology team and made some key shifts in roles, particularly on our senior leadership team, and began laying the foundation for supporting multiple brands. When I envisioned multiple brands, I definitely wanted to leverage the efficiencies and economies of scale of having certain functions that were shared by all brands—buying the services in a chargeback manner based upon usage—such as human resources, finance, marketing, franchise sales, learning and development, clinical support, and technology. During the year, we promoted three vice presidents to senior vice presidents and built detailed two-to-three-year plans for their opportunity to move to C-level positions (i.e., CFO, CMO, etc.).

We also increased our investment in human resources with an upgrade in talent from a manager to an assistant vice president of human resources, recognizing the higher-level skills needed in the role to support succession planning and a stock option plan. We have had minimal (less than 5 percent) turnover of our top and/or not easily replaceable employees in the past three years. That said, with an improving economy we want to ensure that we can dedicate more time and resources to employee development, so we maintain a low turnover rate for our employees who are exceeding expectations.

The additions and/or changes for the year included the following.

FRANCHISEE SUPPORT ADDITIONS/CHANGES:

With the investments in 2008 and 2009, no further positions were added in 2010.

TECHNOLOGY ADDITIONS/CHANGES:

We doubled the technology department by adding the following positions in 2010: a vice president of technology (promoted to senior vice president before the end of the year), a project manager, four developers, and a second quality assurance analyst.

ADMINISTRATION ADDITIONS AND/OR CHANGES:

After the large incremental additions in 2008 and 2009, we made no additional hires and also reduced one member of the senior leadership team related to restructuring franchise sales.

SUMMARY:

At the end of the year we had 51 employees, including J.D. and me, supporting 140 franchisees. We added seven during the year but had a net employee count gain during the year of six after the restructuring of franchise sales.

By the end of our fifth year, our 51 employees were aligned by department or function as follows:

FRANCHISEE SUPPORT:

+ Sixteen domestic franchisee-dedicated positions across field support, BrightStart, national accounts, preopening, and the support center (or one employee for every nine franchisees and every 12 locations). The size of this group and their breadth of talent are engaged holistically to constantly improve franchisee unit economics. For some franchisees, this will mean additional resources and/or support are required, and for others proactive support to transfer out of the system by selling their business. With shared goals among these employees centered on continuous improvement in franchisee performance, the cross-functional team is working together to offer the right type of support at the right time to achieve the best outcome for the franchisees.

+ One dedicated international operations director

TECHNOLOGY:

+ 14 in technology

ADMINISTRATION:

+ 5 in franchise sales
+ 11 in finance/administrative/executive/human resources/contract administration/learning and development
+ 4 in marketing

We embraced the magic wand and invested heavily in support. I use the word *invested* because we consider adding staff an investment, not just an incremental expense. It was certainly a leap of faith, but we soon began to see that we made the right choices. We had revenues per dollar of payroll higher than those of most of our peer group, as shown in the audited financial statements included in every franchisor's filed FDD. That came about because we were helping our franchisees drive higher revenues, so our revenues rose in turn. We see greater opportunities to accelerate our franchisees' results and our own with the large number of technology enhancements that will be completed in 2011.

2010 RECAP:

Open Locations:

+ 198

Open Franchisees:

+ 140

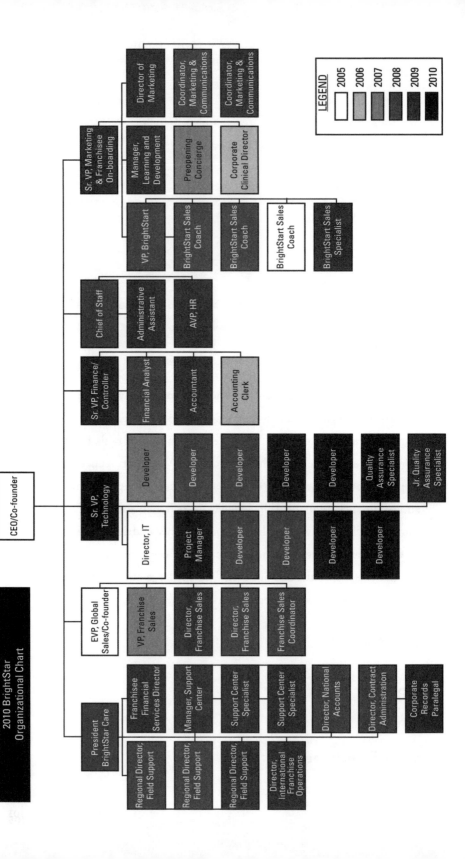

2010 BrightStar Organizational Chart

LEGEND
2005
2006
2007
2008
2009
2010

Staff Hired:

+ 6 (total staff: 51)

Functions Outsourced:

+ Legal is fully outsourced. Expected partially in house 2012.

End-of-Year Organization by Category:

+ Franchisee support: 17 (16 domestic and 1 international)
+ Technology: 14
+ Administration: 20

2010 Key Metrics:*

+ Revenue per $ of payroll: $2.37 (improvement; 2011 projected above $3.50)
+ Revenue per employee: $233,603 (improvement; 2011 projected above $350,000)
+ EBITDA per employee: $53,762 (doubling over 2009; 2011 projected $150,000)
+ EBITDA as % of revenues: 23% (doubling over 2009; 2011 projected 40%+)

*Costs for director, international operations, and revenues from international expansion excluded.

Linking Pay to Performance

The ability to inspire a team is critical in the early years because you don't have excess dollars to drive performance through monetary reward. Actually, I don't believe that money is what drives employees, as long as they feel they are compensated fairly for what is asked of them. This is at the crux of building a great team.

That said, however, you get what you pay for. Just as you can't buy a Lexus for the price of a Taurus, it is equally unlikely you will get and retain an A-level player for D-level compensation.

Compensation Philosophy

At BrightStar we benchmark wages annually and subscribe to resources such as FRANdata's Annual Compensation Study, which provides the low, average, median, and high wages and total compensation for the most common franchise positions. We decentralize our BrightStart and field support teams to have them nearer to their franchisees and reduce travel times and costs. This philosophy makes the regional data available in compensation studies less relevant to us, but for those systems that require all personnel to work from the corporate office, then regional or local pay data will be an important data point to evaluate. The study also breaks down those figures by food and non-food categories and by the size of the franchise system. We want to make sure we have our star players at the high end of the compensation range. With our average field support director's salary double the median recorded in the FRANdata Annual Compensation Study for non-food, we get what we pay for—an average of 15 or more years of experience and experience in franchising, staffing, or home care.

I don't believe in across-the-board merit increases or one-size-fits-all investments in professional development. I believe that A-level players have demonstrated their ability to contribute, and they have gone the extra mile by meeting every deadline and exceeding every goal. This high-quality talent is a critical part of our success. A-level players should make up 20 to 30 percent (hopefully) of the employees in most organizations. I recommend directing company funds toward these top employees—both for increased compensation and professional development.

It's okay to not increase the salaries or invest in the professional development of average players or lower-performing players. This frees up more money for the high performers. If you factor a 3 percent increase in wages into a budget, then a handful may get 10+ percent increases and double that number may get 0 to 2 percent to offset it. Every employee has the opportunity to hit his goals and meet his deadlines; when everyone does, I will be thrilled to increase the wages by a lot more than 3 percent. In a performance-based culture, you are rewarded on results, not tenure, popularity, or likability. Some employees thrive in this culture, but others don't because they are not accustomed to this degree of accountability.

Driving and Rewarding Results Through Accountability

We have a specific process in place to ensure that collectively, as an organization, we have identified our A-level players. Annually, sometimes more often, the senior leadership group force ranks the entire organization. We invest heavily in the top 20 percent with formal succession planning, professional development investments, and increased stock options (we will discuss these later in this section). We review for each employee what possible career paths could be available and match that with the employee's interests. We then assess the hard skill and soft skill "gaps" and build a plan and allocate dollars for the employee to remove the gaps to prepare for the next role. We have several success stories where quantifiable goals were defined that an employee could achieve to move to the next level. I may have expected one employee to take 12 to 18 months, but because she knew the opportunity, she drove harder and faster to accomplish the goals (resulting in significant increases in leads for our franchisees and new business) in six to eight months. We also have committed to a plan by which, as our revenue per dollar of payroll exceeds $4.50, we will extend formal succession planning and professional development programs further into the organization, reaching our top 50 percent.

To build a culture of shared success, you have to decide whether you are willing to share your profits with the entire organization. Employees are often supportive of decisions to not receive bonuses (that doesn't mean they have to like it) when they see that the company didn't achieve its goals (i.e., meet or exceed its budget). Your employees have to know that they and the company are in it together. In the early years when we had financial losses, we didn't give bonuses. Once we began growing royalties, we looked for opportunities to implement bonus programs to share Bright-Star's financial success.

Bonus Programs

In 2008 we achieved full-year budget goals and paid annual bonuses to all employees based on each employee's position in the company's hierarchy. The same bonus program was in place in 2009, when we did not reach our budget goals, and no bonuses were paid. That decision, while executed according to the budget policy, tested the company culture collectively and our employees individually as to whether they were committed for the long term or the short term.

In 2010 we invested extensive time in researching and building an accountability-based bonus program that calculated and paid bonuses quarterly. Bonuses were variable, based upon the extent to which the company achieved its budget profitability. We used a good, better, and best budget approach, in which revenue goals increased between levels (details about this budgeting approach are covered in chapter 8). Each employee has four goals, each worth 25 percent of the bonus opportunity, with two that can be accomplished individually and two that are shared with others—amongst the department or between departments.

Line employees and managers have equal opportunity in this program, the amount increases for directors and VPs equally, and again, at senior leadership levels, the amounts increase. The program comprises two individual goals and two department goals that are mutually agreed upon by the employee and manager (and then are reviewed and approved or sent back for revision by the senior leadership team). This motivates your A-level players in particular—no matter what their position in the company—because their engagement level to meet goals directly results in their earning potential. Frequently we see the dollars paid to a few line employees exceed those paid to directors, VPs, and, occasionally, a member of the senior leadership team.

In our accountability-based bonus program, goals are selected that increase franchisee revenues and/or decrease franchisee and corporate expenses, or improve franchisee satisfaction (which is the best way to increase the sales of new franchises), thus meeting the company's budget.

BENEFITS PACKAGE

In addition to ensuring that we are paying at or above the higher end of the salary scale for top performers and offering a lucrative quarterly bonus opportunity when the company does well, we look for other ways to share the company's financial success. For example, in August 2010 we increased our health insurance employer contribution, which increased our monthly cost of health insurance by $5,000 per month. We increased the contribution for employees to 70 percent (up from a flat amount based on position within the company) and added a contribution toward spouses/partners and children for the first time ever, of 50 percent. We also decreased the time period required before the company's contribution to our 401(k) program kicks in, beginning January 1, 2011, and in January 2011, the short-term bonus pool opportunity for the "good" budget results was doubled.

STOCK OPTIONS

In 2010, we reorganized all of our entities under a C Corporation in preparation for the launch of our stock option plan in January 2011. I asked each member of my senior leadership team to pick his or her "Top 10" in the entire company, to force-rank within his or her own departments, and to rate as a T, M, or B all other employees. For every employee in the organization, we would know if each was or was not a "Top 10," how each was rated as a T, M, or B, and how department managers force-ranked each of their people. The T (top) designates top performers who are critical to the organization and whose replacement would take approximately one year to perform at or near their level. The M (middle) designates solid performers whose replacement could be functional within six months. The B (bottom) designates those whose replacement could quickly get up to speed within a month.

I assign stock options to all employees based on our high-performance, high-reward culture. As with bonuses, sometimes line employees have more options than their managers, and some directors have more options than VPs. The achievement of quarterly goals under the quarterly bonus program, to recognize those who achieved a higher percentage of their goals, and the rankings were used to determine the initial number of options granted to each employee. Again, since there is an opportunity to award future stock options, with the consent of our board of directors, both new employees and existing employees who increase their contribution or their role within the organization have continued opportunity to share in the potential increase in the value of the enterprise, as we may consider an initial public offering in the future.

The valuation was made as of December 31, 2010, by an independent third party recommended by our law firm. Future valuations, prior to any IPO, will be made using the same methodology. This program allows employees to have an opportunity to share in an IPO event when or if our valuation is higher than when they received options, without having tax consequences until they actually take action to buy the underlying shares (which is known as exercising the option).

SUCCESSION PLANNING

We prepare a formal succession plan for our "Top 10" to help them objectively see exactly what is needed for their future roles. In addition, our top performers receive a professional development investment allocation to build the skills necessary for them to perform future roles. We are investing heavily in the professional development of these employees, including IFA's Certified Franchise Executive certification. We are planning to allocate additional dollars once the company's productivity reaches $4.50 of revenues for each dollar of payroll (selected based upon its correlation to when we will achieve EBITDA as a percentage of revenues of 60 percent, considered by those I network and benchmark with as the best practice standard) to perform this formal succession planning for another 15 employees, bringing the total to 25 employees, nearly 50 percent of the organization.

BRIGHT IDEA:

Ultimately the goal of building a high-performance, highly accountable organization is to build a culture in which employees are empowered and rewarded as owners.

I want my employees to be able to execute our plans without needing or wanting me to approve each step. If an employee needs to wait for her boss's approval, a bottleneck is inevitable. You need to make sure that all employees understand your strategy and your budget goals and then empower them to make the decisions and take the actions to deliver those results.

Weed Out Poor Performance

Equally important—quite frankly, this is even more important—is the review of the bottom 20 percent. This is critical for two reasons: First, top performers don't want to work alongside or be held back by weak performers. If you don't weed out the employees who are missing deadlines, exhibiting poor attitudes, pushing work to other departments, and not meeting goals, your A-level players will either (a) get fed up and leave or (b) stop performing like A-level players. Second, employees who do not fit into your high-performance culture will be happier and fit better elsewhere. In any event, you and your organization will be better off without them. I say this because we all want to be nice, especially to those we like, but leadership isn't about being nice. It's about being able to make the tough decisions that are for the "good of the whole."

Annually, I look long and hard at the employees noted as "B" (bottom) performers and ask myself and my senior team if the organization would be better without those individuals. If the answer is yes, clearly they need to go. I review my senior team in the same way twice a year, rather than annually, because a weak link or bad culture fit in leadership can derail the entire organization if left to fester.

Another important question to ask in evaluating your "B" players is whether you would hire an individual again for the same compensation you are currently paying him.

The real key is to make improvements so that the number of employees who don't meet one or both of these tests declines year to year. For example, at the end of 2009, we had five employees who were assigned a "B" (bottom) rating *and* had failed both of these tests. We took steps to remove them from the organization (after meticulously documenting poor performance and missed deadlines), and they were gone a year later. At the end of 2010, we had a strong organization rowing together with only one employee who was designated a "B" *and* failing both tests. The important distinction is that being a "B" in and of itself is not bad, as there are many roles that contribute to the organization but still could be transitioned to a new employee relatively easily (or in less than one month).

The organization has become stronger due to at least three personnel development strategies: (1) We have hired better as we focused on hiring for attitude and assessing for skills that we will need in two years; (2) we are investing in our talent with better bonus programs, benefits, and stock options; and (3) we have built a culture aligned together, with 50 percent of the bonus opportunity being tied to shared goals with other employees (within or among different departments). Employees are rowing together to not let one another down. Employees prioritize the shared goals and have a higher achievement rate on them than they have in the other 50 percent that are individual goals. This has built camaraderie. The bonus program design is discussed more fully in chapter 8 to assist you in considering a program with equal weighting between individual and shared goals to build accountability while also building a team culture.

Closing Thoughts

Early on we invested heavily in the infrastructure, and now we are beginning to grow into our capacity. We will continue to add field support positions annually and a few key positions here and there. We made the hard choice in 2008 and 2009 to add 17 and 18 positions, respectively, when most others were downsizing because of the weakened economy. We pushed forward to increase the tools and support we could make available to our franchisees.

We have begun laying the foundation to support additional brands. We thought this through from multiple vantage points in 2010 when we realized that within three years (by 2013) we would be sold out domestically in the BrightStar Care brand because all territories would be sold or committed to as part of a development agreement. In a mature brand, we wouldn't be able to keep departments such as franchise sales, learning and development, BrightStart, and preopening, since they serve franchisees only at the beginning of our relationship or only occasionally. Only by adding future brands that require each of these shared functions, which are engaged most of the time, can we make these same shared functions available on the rare occasions when our BrightStar Care franchisees need them. For example, if a franchisee wanted or needed to sell her business, she would need help from the franchise sales team, and if she had employee turnover, she would need learning and development to train the new team member. By continuing to plan ahead for future growth through new brands, we retain exceptional talent and ensure that our franchisees will have available the resources they need, though very infrequently, when they need them.

•　•　•

An organization is only as good as its people. Our team is the single biggest factor in our success. Whether you choose to franchise your business or not, you have learned some key guiding principles on attracting, developing, and retaining top performers. You learned how to implement a process to continually upgrade the talent of your organization. You probably have a great team in place, but these examples will hopefully help ensure that you remain focused on this critical priority. With a great team, it is important to focus on engaging and retaining them by driving and rewarding accountability.

CHAPTER 5

Building Your External Team

My entrepreneurial outlook was shaped in 2002 when I read *Rich Dad, Poor Dad* by Robert Kiyosaki and Sharon L. Lechter (2000), after which J.D. and I attended one of his conferences. The conference forever influenced my concept of the power of a strong team—both internal and external. Robert had an amazing partner who he had brought on to help him dramatically expand; he had an amazing event coordinator; and he had a host of advisors-consultants to whom we had access and who really added a lot to the conference from a content perspective. The key to Robert's real success, as he himself acknowledged, was the strength of the team he had formed.

I knew that over time our success would similarly be enabled, enhanced, and sustained through building a strong team, both internally and externally. In the previous chapter we looked at the key elements of building and retaining a strong internal team. In this chapter I want to hit on a few key areas where an external team can create a breakthrough: (1) form and leverage a board of advisors; (2) find and utilize functional experts to bridge the gap where you don't have as much experience in managing; and (3) build strong supplier relationships for what you buy and what your franchisees need to purchase. BrightStar's external team created a strategic advantage for us.

Form and Leverage a Board of Advisors

You may already have a board of advisors for your existing (company-owned) business. First, you may be asking what the difference is between a board of advisors and a board of directors and when you would use one versus the other. A board of directors generally is a voting group that helps direct the organization and is the group to whom the CEO reports. A board of directors is necessary for publicly traded companies and is also common if you have outside investors. A board of directors makes decisions and therefore takes risks in its actions, so the board members need to be protected with directors and officers insurance coverage—which can be expensive.

Since we are privately owned and have no legal reason to have a voting board of directors (other than me, as the sole managing member of our LLC and sole shareholder of our C Corporation), I formed a board of advisors to provide me with a group of individuals to help me improve on the results and strategy for the business. You might consider establishing a board of advisors if you have no legal need for a board of directors with outside directors and therefore lack outside help in evolving your company and identifying and planning for outside opportunities and threats. This group should be focused on the franchising initiative and have specific franchising experience to offer you when you are ready to franchise your business. Building a board of advisors who have the expertise that you lack will multiply your capacity for thinking through the best ways to grow. You know your business and your industry. You do not yet know franchising.

Two of the most important ingredients in selecting a board of advisors are (1) that the group understands your size at start-up and the path you are on to become a bigger company, and (2) that each board member aligns with you from a values perspective. You need board members who put you and the success of your organization as a high priority.

When I first began thinking about franchising, I was fortunate to discover a program called Athena Power Link. This program helps female business owners reach new levels of success by providing them with a board of advisors free for one year. The program selects five or six advisors to serve on the board and trains mentees on how to prepare for board meetings and utilize board members individually and collectively. I enjoyed this experience from late 2004 to late 2005, during which time there were a few hard lessons to learn.

AVOID THIS PITFALL:
One of the hard lessons I learned was that I should be extremely cautious in hiring a consultant who was also already an advisory board member.

We did not yet know one another well, nor did I have much experience with the dynamics of a board. Though many around me warned that the consultant in question might have had an ulterior motive, I wouldn't believe that this person wanted anything more than a potential full-time job with our company. I became somewhat dependent on this person, and then this person tried to come between J.D. and me as co-founders and demanded a third ownership of our company without any intention of putting in any cash.

The second hard lesson came at about the same time, when a franchise attorney on the board suggested that I work with his partner, offering me a "huge price break" because I was just getting started.

AVOID THIS PITFALL:
Always screen board members and negotiate with them just as much as you would with any other third party.

I was naïve and did not shop around and compare offerings from all possible suppliers of the same service. My "discount" resulted in overpaying by at least $75,000 when I compared what I would have paid either of my next two law firms. The hard lessons, though, are where I learn the best, so I set out some rules when I formed my own board of advisors.

Your board members will be in a unique position to have complete access to you and your organization's proprietary information, so you will want to have confidentiality agreements in place and choose advisors who do not have ownership in any competing businesses. While it is not uncommon for a business owner to ask an existing vendor or consultant to serve on the board of advisors, I do not recommend hiring or beginning to buy services from a board member and then keeping that individual as a board member. It will be difficult to treat such individuals as you would any other vendor (if, for instance, they solicit you to do business or for a job) and it will be difficult to be confrontational with them to negotiate with them, so it's better to steer clear from the beginning.

I formed my own (non–Power Link sponsored) board of advisors in 2006 with advisors that I selected. I determined to have a board with an odd number of members. (A board of advisors is a non-voting group, but you may on occasion want to take a count of the various positions, and an odd number prevents a tie.) I first sought a franchise attorney and had the good fortune of hearing a brilliant one, who also had great business acumen, speak at a Franchise Update Media Group's annual Franchise Leadership & Development Conference. I wanted him on my team in any capacity he would offer to be until I could afford to hire him. Another member was a banker who had been on my original Athena Power Link panel. I also sought two local area franchisors—one who was a working mother at the time she had expanded her brand internationally and had 25 years of experience, and another who had been franchising for only a few years and thus would clearly remember the bumps and bruises of the early stage. The last person I approached was an executive from one of the largest franchise systems in the world who had just begun consulting. Every one of my advisors was willing to help me. I simply asked and they said yes. They had been successful, remembered their struggles or those of others, and wanted to help me. Many liked feeling a part of something that would make a difference (creating businesses and/or healthcare) or liked being part of helping a business grow without having to roll up their sleeves again to do the work.

During that inaugural year the majority of the board members contacted me privately to wisely suggest replacing a particular board member whose experience lay with a very large franchisor and whose input therefore was not useful to me at such an early stage of franchising. Just as with employees, you will most likely need to replace board members as your need for different skill sets changes or if they no longer have the time to contribute. I met with the board member privately, and he graciously acknowledged that it was difficult to provide relevant advice for the start-up phase of a franchise compared to what he had seen offered by the multibillion-dollar franchise company where he had worked.

Let me mention here that I didn't pay my initial board of advisors because we were in the launching phase and didn't have much money. They knew that when I could afford to pay them I would. BrightStar provided lunch and reimbursed travel for each of the four annual meetings in the first few years. As we became profitable, each board member received $500 per meeting attended. I also looked to increase my board of advisors as we grew and faced new opportunities. In 2010, for example, I added the president of another franchise company, who is an expert in consumer marketing. I recommend seeking others to help you in areas where you do not have the expertise as you expand your organization. (For other resources to supplement your knowledge base, see the section titled "Find and Utilize Functional Experts" later in this chapter.)

My board was very supportive and challenged my thinking, but I knew

I wasn't leveraging them as much as I could. I had experience presenting to a board of directors in my corporate life, but I had never had to run the meeting or been ultimately accountable to a board, so I needed to develop this skill set. At the IFA's Executive Leadership Conference in October 2009, the guru of managing boards himself, Ram Charan, was one of our speakers. I began putting the key ideas from Ram's book, *Boards That Deliver* (Jossey-Bass, 2005) to work, including ensuring that the board clearly understood our strategy, our brand positioning, and our competitive landscape as well as defining the information they needed to advise me better. In addition, I committed to presetting the agenda for the full year, using the main topics from the book such as strategy, organizational structure and evolution, information, competitive assessment, and succession planning. I also increased my frequency of communication to include a monthly e-mail listing of the key activities that had occurred in the prior month, so the board was well informed about the changes in the organization and were ready to hit the ground running at the board meetings. These changes really made—and continue to make—a huge difference in our overall effectiveness.

BRIGHT IDEA:
I believe so strongly in the value of having a board of advisors that we recommend the same practice to our franchisees and provide them with an instructional video to assist them in forming their own boards.

Though I don't think any of our board members would ever use knowledge of BrightStar's proprietary intellectual property and secret business initiatives in a way that was not in the company's best interest, we nevertheless use a non-compete and confidentiality agreement specifically crafted for a board of advisors. It is simply good business practice to protect against any potential harm, just as it is good practice to have non-compete and confidentiality agreements signed by employees (where allowed by state law) and social media policy guidelines signed or acknowledged by both employees and franchisees. It is better to be safe than sorry.

We have benefited from having a few trusted franchisees as informal advisors, too. Before you get too far along in the process, discuss with this small group of franchisees a communication or a new program and gauge how it will be received by all franchisees. You will also be able to confide in these franchisees to gauge how pending employee changes will impact and be interpreted by other franchisees.

Find and Utilize Functional Experts

I have a CPA background, so I understand finances and banking. As the CEO in my organization, however, I must also manage other key support areas such as technology and human resources. To handle these areas well—speaking the same language and accomplishing what needs to be accomplished—I have needed a "translator" to help me ask the right questions and set the right expectations in these areas.

BRIGHT IDEA:

In each area where you do not have prior experience and therefore cannot adequately evaluate the performance of those you manage, you should learn enough to do so or hire a consultant/advisor to help you.

I didn't begin using these resources until after we had nearly 100 franchisees, when we were nearing royalty self-sufficiency. Although I could have started working with one or two consultants a year earlier, and wish I had, experts are expensive. But the ROI is high and this investment is critical to reach true scalability and success.

Had I learned this lesson earlier, I would have made smarter investments in technology and been able to develop our technology department much sooner. Fortunately, at the 2008 IFA Executive Leadership Conference I met Scott Klososky (www.Klososky.com), an expert in the technology field. Scott has extensive experience in growing many successful businesses, and he knows that the two disciplines—business and technology—are sometimes at odds. I hired Scott to help me evaluate our technology tools and our team to ensure that I had the necessary ingredients to build a world-class technology platform and innovate our business by leveraging technology.

I had also never directly managed human resources and realized I also needed a "Scott" in this area to help me learn and to assess what we were doing well and, most important, what we needed to add or improve. I hired a human resources consultant recommended by my strategic coach, and we bridged the gap by ramping up my knowledge and ability to hold the leader accountable and help her with succession planning and development.

I am likewise now working with a strategic coach on a regular basis. However, this is different from my examples of hiring consultants in technology and human resources because strategy is my greatest strength. (This was confirmed when I read Tom Rath's *StrengthsFinder 2.0* [Gallup Press, 2007]. I highly recommend this online test to any manager in any organization, as it focuses on how to encourage, develop, and utilize every individual's strong suits for better performance.) *StrengthsFinder 2.0* defines my #2 strength as relating to others, by the way—hence the hugging.

So, if I know how to be strategic, why do I have a strategic coach? Just being able to see trends and invest in external information and take the time to review how this information may impact our business model does not mean that the best solutions can be identified alone. A great strategic coach will ask questions to challenge your thinking to help you evolve your ideas to even greater heights. It is hard for us as leaders to spend time thinking about and formulating strategy. The focus here is not on the best way to execute strategy for the organization, but to build in the resources to ensure that you are spending time on strategy. We will always find time for the tactical because, quite frankly, it's more fun to cross items off a list than to spend hours "thinking" without necessarily having anything right away to show for it.

Great strategic coaches are best defined by their ability to formulate great questions so that you and your team can develop better strategies and own them. These coaches don't provide the strategy—they are building a capability and facilitating a process to help the team get to the strategy. One of the best decisions I ever made was to recognize the capabilities of our Women Presidents' Organization facilitator and begin working with her in 2008 on our strategy. We eventually brought our senior leadership team into the process and still later a broader team of about 30 people, including all field support and BrightStart members and all managers and above from every area of the company.

With a strong board of advisors, a couple of franchisees as confidants and sounding boards, a few strong external team members to supplement your knowledge in areas you are less familiar with, and a dedicated commitment to strategy through a strategic coach, you are ready to focus on developing strong relationships with your suppliers.

Build Strong Supplier Relationships

You will need suppliers for the services you require as the franchisor and for the products and services your franchisees will need. The stronger your relationships with your key suppliers, the better. Ultimately, you want to work with suppliers who will look for new and innovative ways to add value to you, but you should realize that they will go to this level of effort only if they know you value them beyond the next transaction. Our suppliers are so much more than providers of services—they are constantly on the lookout for opportunities for us. You will have an opportunity at IFA events to meet good suppliers that are knowledgeable about franchising and to ask other franchisors what suppliers they are using.

Franchisor Suppliers

In the very beginning, you will be well served to use suppliers who are experts in their field and who will deliver a higher quality output than you may be able to do on your own. For example, I would recommend working with an expert to design all training content, from the operations manuals to the training curriculum, to make sure that you structure them correctly and that they are user-friendly. If you have never worked with an expert to revise your operations manuals, any time is the right time, but the sooner you can upgrade the better—and this will spare you the expense of hiring a full-time employee or spending your own time to generate material that may not be as effective.

One of the best suppliers I ever selected and still happily use today is Fishman Public Relations. Regrettably, I overspent in the beginning by hiring a big national public relations (PR) firm that said they understood franchising but didn't. It is critical to have a PR firm that understands franchising and that is actively involved in the IFA. At some point, you may have so many local PR opportunities that you will need a second PR resource for local franchisee PR support.

In the world of franchisor PR and national PR opportunities for the brand, I couldn't be happier with our choice of Fishman Public Relations. Brad and Sherri Fishman are very active in franchising and attend nearly every IFA event. Both of them took me under their wing, helping me meet key people in the industry and securing national coverage for us in the *Wall Street Journal*, *Entrepreneur* magazine, *Crain's*, and on Fox Business Network. Brad and Sherri became great mentors and were passionate about helping my brand succeed. They went the extra mile to help me network in franchising and to deliver ROI with our public relations dollars, both in finding new franchisees and in helping our franchisees get new customers.

Franchisee Suppliers

The range of suppliers you will contract with on behalf of your franchisees will vary widely based on your industry. Vendors that understand franchising work with two customers: the franchisor and the franchisee. The vendors that have not been able to progress with us as we grew did not service franchising and/or they declined to become involved with the IFA to learn franchising and to leverage it as a way to expand their business.

Franchisors generally will have much greater success in negotiating for the quality and pricing with suppliers than individual franchisees will. To execute this strategy, a franchisor needs to be able to leverage the supply chain framework laid out in Item 8 of the FDD, the section that describes the approved supplies, products, and/or services that a franchisee must buy through an identified third party or through the franchisor.

We actually took a financial risk in our earlier stages, trying to do the right thing for our franchisees by committing to large print volumes to get their individual order prices reduced. This usually isn't a big deal as long as you continue with the same supplier, but sometimes you outgrow a particular supplier and must move on. We were fortunate in 2010 to find a great new printer. It is a decision not to be taken lightly, and I would advise you to evaluate early the types of clients that any supplier is servicing. Does the supplier service franchisors and do these franchisors have thousands of locations? You do not want to be the supplier's largest client at some point and have to change because they cannot handle the volume.

AVOID THIS PITFALL:

Changing printers is difficult on everyone involved and expensive, so do your homework and make your decision the right one, the first time.

In many cases, franchisees can get their Uncle Phil or some other relative to print brochures and produce promotional items with the logo for cheaper prices. The franchisor's primary role, however, is to protect the brand, and that means balancing quality and price so that customers see only high quality. Of course, mandating quality will cause the price to be higher than if there are no quality standards in place.

BRIGHT IDEA:

Franchisors should select and mandate the use of any suppliers who will assist in positively and consistently presenting the image of the brand.

Another supplier relationship that franchisors should absolutely foster involves access to financing. Up until 2008, franchisors could remain uninvolved in the franchisees' need to access financing because home equity loans and small business loans were readily available. Times have since changed, and every franchisor must realize that the only way to continue to grow is to continually develop, nurture, and promote financing sources for their franchisees. We have taken a very active role in presenting our business model to multiple lenders and trying to streamline the process for our franchisees as much as possible. There are great supplier relationships that can assist with this: For example, in our first year we ensured that our brand was on the SBA Franchise Registry. Administered by FRANdata, the process includes an FDD review to ensure that all provisions meet the guidelines for the underlying business to be eligible for SBA financing. As soon as we learned about Bank Credit Reports, we began ordering them for our brand. A Bank Credit Report is a brand-specific evaluation that details the key areas of growth and risk for the brand, its competitors, and the industry as a whole that bankers are concerned about. We have used them for years with banks to assist franchisees with access to financing. (Both the SBA Franchise Registry and the Bank Credit Reports are available through FRANdata.)

We were the first franchisor approved for a credit facility through Franchise America Finance, which makes SBA financing available to start-up or expanding franchisees. The credit facility allowed us to know that there was money set aside for our franchisees and allowed us and our franchisees to know the conditions necessary to be approved, including credit score, liquidity, and net worth. We have taken an active role in making financing available to our franchisees, including adding a position to our franchisee support team. Since most franchisees don't "speak banker," we hired an ex-banker with franchise operations experience to bridge the communication between bankers and the franchisees, and to assist in the challenge of accessing limited available capital.

Ron Feldman, the founder of Franchise America Finance, says that "in today's capital access environment, when franchisees are seeking financing, your FDD is not your friend." You need a lawyer who understands that there is potential growing tension between providing useful business information about franchise systems to lenders and to prospective franchisees, and that separate rules may apply to each of those groups. You need a compliant process to provide information *directly* to banks in a format that they need to make lending decisions—they want more than what is in most franchisors' FDDs (especially since most franchisors still do not include any Item 19 information in their FDDs). Also keep in mind that, because of regulations regarding financial performance information, you are unable to provide any financial performance information to a prospective franchisee beyond what is in Item 19 of the FDD. Your franchise lawyer should understand how important it is to assist you in finding a solution to this dilemma.

You will have numerous suppliers for areas such as payroll processing, credit card processing, office supplies, computer equipment, job boards for hiring, etc. Regardless of the product or service your system requires, the approach you take to ensure the best quality and pricing for your franchisees can be enhanced by following these guidelines:

+ Spend time helping suppliers understand your vision so you can pre-negotiate volume discounts for a declining pricing structure as you achieve certain volume levels. This prenegotiation will also mean that you won't have to keep going back to the supplier as your volume increases, because the next one to two years of projected volume levels were already prenegotiated.
+ Secure a most-favored-nations clause to ensure that any other companies ordering the same volume are not getting a better price than you are.
+ Mandate that any franchisee-requested modification of the product or service is submitted to the franchisor for preapproval to keep control over system standards.

Take a methodical approach in securing supplier relationships that includes identifying all the types of goods and services your franchisees are buying and then prioritizing them based on the estimated amount being spent by the entire system on each of these. Begin working your way through the list by starting with the highest dollars spent. By doing so, you are likely to be more successful in achieving price reductions for volume and, in turn, having the biggest impact in improving your franchisees' bottom line. I've also found it prudent to put key supplier contracts that impact the franchisees' profitability out to bid every two years—not necessarily to move the relationship, but to assure that we have fair prices for the volume our system is ordering.

Closing Thoughts

Building a strong team is the key to a solid business. In this chapter we reviewed some key ways to expand your thinking about the team to include the external players: your board of advisors, functional experts, and suppliers. Seek board members whose expertise complements your own and who will ask the tough questions to help your business grow. Functional experts can fill in your gaps of knowledge and make you a much stronger, well-rounded leader. Selecting suppliers in the franchise industry has nuances that selecting suppliers in other industries do not. Franchise suppliers must understand and be able to effectively service two customers simultaneously: the franchisor and the franchisee.

. . .

You now know you need to have a strong foundation in place with a world-class FDD and team to begin selling your franchise opportunity. In the next section, we will walk through how to build a sales process, how to implement technology to streamline that process, and how to find potential franchisees and screen them so you select the best for your system.

SECTION 3

BUILDING THE FRANCHISE FAMILY

CHAPTER 6

Implementing an Effective Franchise Sales Process

You have multiple company-owned locations showing that your concept could be successfully replicated in additional locations or territories, and you have your franchise disclosure document (FDD) and financing in place. What do you need now? Franchisees, of course!

While recruiting franchisees is important to growth, it is also important to note that the offer and sale of franchises is highly regulated. You should consult with your franchise attorney as you design your sales process, including, among other things, how you will handle franchise validation (in which prospects ask franchisees about their experience), your review of the prospects' business plans, and other critical aspects of the sales process. The key is to understand the legal do's and don'ts of franchise sales, as you want to ensure that, while your process enables prospects to gain the information they need, they gain it in a way that complies with legal requirements. I highly encourage that you make every effort to have a robust Item 19 in your FDD, as this has helped us tremendously in the processes that we have built, because we already *legally* share so much financial performance information with prospective franchisees. In addition, you should have everyone involved in the franchise sales process—including senior management who may be involved in Join-the-Team Day (discussed later in this chapter)—attend franchise sales compliance training, especially the IFA's FranGuard program.

I struggled with which chapter should come first: the one on lead generation or the one on sales process—the chicken, as the proverb goes, or the egg? It doesn't do any good to get leads and then have a bad sales process. Conversely, it doesn't do any good to have a great sales process and inadequate leads. In both the design of the sales process and the generation of leads, the consideration of the target franchisee (one who would find value in your business and has the qualities that you believe are necessary to succeed in your business) is critical. (We will discuss the profile of your ideal franchisee in the beginning of chapter 7.) In the end I chose to begin with discussing how to design a great sales process and incorporating into that discussion a few important subtopics: (1) utilizing experts and technology for optimal solutions; (2) mapping the sales process; (3) leveraging sales personnel (including the number of salespeople needed based on your lead flow as well as the benefits of a sales qualifier); and (4) evaluating key franchise sales metrics to assess how the process is performing.

Throughout this chapter and the next one, I use terms commonly heard within the industry. We use Process Peak, a technology platform, for our franchise sales process. This system refers to potential franchisees seeking information about our organization before we qualify them as a "suspect." Those who complete our longer confidential questionnaire (CQ) are referred to as a "lead." In the industry, however, both would be referred to as leads. The differentiation, however, is crucial for evaluating key metrics.

Therefore, to avoid confusion, I will use the following three categories when referring to those individuals who are evaluating our opportunity:

- *suspects* for everyone, regardless of qualification
- *CQ lead* for all those interested in our concept who have completed our confidential questionnaire and are therefore a qualified lead
- *completion* for all closed sales

Candidates and *prospects* are used interchangeably to refer to someone considering a franchise opportunity. Once they sign a franchise agreement, they are referred to as a *franchisee.*

Utilize Experts and Technology

We were fortunate to select 175 franchisees and to sign over 250 franchise agreements (we have more franchise agreements than franchisees, as our multi-unit franchisees sign agreements for the second or third locations). As you look at setting your own goals for franchise sales, you will want to understand how what you require of your franchisees impacts the number of potential prospects who will meet your criteria. The number of prospects that you may receive typically will decline as your requirements increase in each of the following areas: investment range, liquidity, net worth, credit score, and experience.

We have an investment in the over-$100,000 category. Our required minimum liquidity is $100,000 (according to what franchisees disclose on a financial statement, including cash and stocks). We will count 401(k) if the prospect will be accessing it as a funding source. We require minimum net worth of $500,000 (or $400,000 and a working spouse to cover household expenses) and a minimum credit score of 685 (increased from 600 as we saw bank requirements tighten in 2009).

In 2005–2007, when it was easier to access capital, particularly home equity loans, the net worth requirement was only $250,000, but we increased the amount with the credit access crisis, recognizing that banks required more collateral and significantly discount home equity. Franchise sales are tougher as the investment range of a franchise concept increases because there is a smaller pool of candidates; a candidate for a concept above $100,000, for instance, is much harder to find than one for concepts with a $50,000 to $100,000 investment. The requirements set for net worth, liquidity, and credit score for prospects narrows the funnel further.

As you evaluate what your initial investment will be and the total amount of working capital a franchisee needs until the business reaches cash flow, you need to think about the access to capital environment and what banks will require to finance your franchisee. I recommend setting your internal criteria at or higher than the banks' requirements and within the bounds of three primary considerations that include the following: (1) investment level, (2) the skills and background needed of the franchisee, and (3) the defined culture. The higher the investment level, the greater the required skill, and the more protective you are of your culture, the fewer available candidates you will have.

Many lenders prefer a franchisee to have experience in the industry; a franchisor who does not require such experience of its franchisees will have to demonstrate to the lenders a level of support that overcomes the franchisee's inexperience. Culture, on the other hand, does not have to be a limiting factor, as you can use culture to attract and emotionally engage the right candidate.

I can't stress enough how much a great sales process influences great results. We have had help developing and then enhancing our process repeatedly. Having an outside advisor or consultant review your process for missing pieces is incredibly helpful. We found, for example, that we knew our "story" so well that we were leaving out important passages that a prospect would want and need to know.

We have had great success in developing and/or enhancing our sales process working with two consultants, Joe Mathews and Kurt Landwehr.

We also have had each of them manage our department and/or sell directly for us when we really needed an outside perspective to create our next breakthrough of performance by coaching the team, improving our processes, and increasing our lead flow. A big boost to the sales department came when we moved our sales process to Process Peak, an amazing technology platform, after three years of successfully selling franchises. It allowed us to automate the manual process of sending a binder of information to prospects, drastically reducing our printing and postage costs and eliminating worry about delays in the mail.

With their expertise in blueprinting sales processes, Process Peak personnel combed through our process, pointing out missing information. We were then able to cover this information up front, so that prospects felt better about the process and knew that we were not trying to hide anything. Our close rates nearly doubled within four months of deploying Process Peak. The results and ROI thus speak for themselves.

In addition, the technology platform that the Process Peak system is written on aligns with our technology strategy, because we are building on SharePoint and .net platforms to offer our franchisees and ourselves increased workflow automation, dashboards, and business intelligence tools. This will be—or should be—the direction best-in-class companies are headed toward in the future.

Map the Sales Process

As mentioned in the opening, careful consideration of the franchisee you want to attract is a critical component both in defining the right sales process to engage prospects and in determining the right lead-generation tactics to find them. I will refer to *selling* a lot throughout this section, but I want to emphasize that, although we call it selling, we have a strong philosophy and practice of *selecting* franchisees who also believe we are the right fit for them. The decision to do so is a mutual one. We do not bring just anyone into our family: We require much more than financial qualification in our selection of franchisees. *Who* you allow into your system will play the largest factor in your success or failure as a franchisor.

AVOID THIS PITFALL:

The mistake that many franchisors make in the early years is to sell franchises to almost anyone who is willing to sign the franchise agreement and pay the initial franchise fee.

That approach will hurt you in the long run.

Our system for handling initial contact with a prospect provides an immediate e-mail response when an online request for information is received. Our sales qualifier, a position dedicated to contacting and qualifying prospects and then assigning the qualified prospects to one of our salespeople, then attempts three phone calls and three or four e-mail messages spread out over up to 10 days, with the first contact attempt within four business hours. If she can't reach the prospect, the lead is closed out, and we try to reengage the prospect in an e-mail campaign later.

For those we do contact and who meet our criteria, we provide access to our online virtual brochure, through Process Peak. Prospects are encouraged to go through the first section of information before their initial call with our salesperson. We recognize that buyers are busy and may want to review some information on their own before they are ready to engage in a two-way process (think about the way home buyers look online first to evaluate the homes they are interested in before ever seeking out a real estate agent to set appointments to see these homes). All other steps of the sales process are based upon a mutual give-and-take and engagement on both sides in the process; as such, the other sections of our virtual brochure are password-protected and require our salesperson to be part of the prospect's experience.

BRIGHT IDEA:

We designed homework for the prospect at each stage in our virtual brochure prospect experience and use this to help us determine if the prospect will follow a process.

We also use multiple content formats, including videos, audio, franchisee testimonials, and downloads of information to demonstrate our credibility, including marketing materials, job descriptions, etc.

An ideal process will simultaneously impress and inform a prospect as well as qualify him. Buying a franchise and succeeding at it requires that the franchisee follow the model—including all systems and processes—to reach the desired results. It always shocks me that some franchisees refuse to follow the model. Why in the world invest in a franchise, spend the money, and then not follow the model? Well, for whatever reason, some franchisees do just that. If they won't follow the sales process before they write a check, they most certainly won't follow our business processes after they write the check and join our family. It's better for everyone involved to identify this before they join.

AVOID THIS PITFALL:

Remember: The wrong franchisee is expensive—not only in terms of dollars to support and lost royalty opportunity, but also in terms of the emotional toll and distraction.

So invest your time deeply into getting this process right.

Before jumping into the specific steps of the process, let's review what the process is designed to do. You need to understand why buyers buy businesses so that you can position your business model and establish clearly the value proposition. A buyer needs to feel a "fit" in one or more of three areas with the business she will invest in. First, the buyer will evaluate the concept logically, so the business model needs to make sense (you will need to deliver data, industry level information, unit level economics, ROI, and return on life information to meet this need, all in accordance with the applicable legal requirements, including the Item 19 rules I have referenced previously). Second, the buyer will evaluate the concept in terms of whether she trusts you. The person she will do business with must be credible. Start-up franchisors are marketing the vision of the founder; therefore, the founder must be a big part of the process early on to be credible. As the data you have to share increases, you will need a credible and likable salesperson to tell the franchisor's story. Third, there must be an emotional connection to what the franchisee will be doing. As an example, BrightStar offers an opportunity for a franchisee to make money by making a difference in the lives of families.

The Five-Step Process

How long should your sales process last? It varies, but in general it is fair to say that most buyers who buy businesses, regardless of the level of the franchise investment, do so over a 60- to 90-day period. It is definitely true that time kills deals. To accommodate the five steps in our process, we set an agreed-upon date during a five-to-seven-week time frame for the prospect to decide if he wants to commit to working with us and vice versa.

The steps may vary for you, depending on your concept's level of complexity, and it may change over time—as the model changes or as you improve your processes—as ours has. For our virtual brochure, we break the process into the following five steps: (1) The Opportunity, (2) Competitive Advantages, (3) Training and Support, (4) Validation, and (5) Join-the-Team Day.

STEP ONE: THE OPPORTUNITY

The Opportunity is an introductory section that suspects can access in our virtual brochure prior to their conversation with a salesperson. It does not contain any proprietary information. At the conclusion of this section, the prospect fills out our long CQ so we can evaluate the prospect's fit for our system before we continue.

Prospects at this stage are introduced to the topic of territory selection. Since we are growing fast, we try to have the prospect think about her top three territory choices (rather than just focusing on only one territory) in case her first preference isn't available by the time she reaches the end of the sales process. Once a prospect has submitted her three choices for territory on her CQ, we share the demographic details with her of the three choices as a precursor to step 2. We have our territory availability pre-mapped on MapPoint, and access to it is available to the whole sales team so they know in real time what is available. Our director of contract administration maintains it as new territories are sold. I recommend investing in pre-mapping the United States, using the demographic criteria that are appropriate for your model, and importing this information into MapPoint.

STEP TWO: COMPETITIVE ADVANTAGES

The Competitive Advantages section provides an in-depth look at our differentiators in terms of our breadth of revenue sources, our recruiting and retention strategy, and our technology. Prospects have an incentive to complete the CQ in order to gain access to this section, which contains proprietary information.

At this stage we engage the prospect in a discussion about what she is looking for in a business and mutually evaluate with her whether our business can help her meet her goals. A thorough interview (and active listening) is critical for both the prospect and the franchisor, as it is the best way to ensure that this business is capable of meeting the prospect's financial, lifestyle, and emotional goals and can justify her investment in it. The full sales process takes weeks for both you and the prospect, so devoting a thorough 45 minutes to this interview is worth the effort; it ensures that you both see the possibility of a fit before continuing for weeks and weeks through the rest of the process. For a list of suggested questions to ask of a prospective franchisee, visit www.growsmartriskless.com.

This first call is probably between 60 and 90 minutes, of which 45 minutes are dedicated to the interview and the remainder walks through the information in this section of the virtual brochure. You will deliver enough information for the prospect to evaluate initially if you meet her logical, emotional, and trust parameters. The prospect needs to be able to understand how you will deliver value to her, as opposed to other franchisors, by emphasizing how you are better than her other business choices.

We moved up the introduction to accessing financing sources to step 2 from step 5 in 2010, once we had financing options available and after recognizing that prospects had become apprehensive about their ability to access capital and about the delays associated with accessing capital. As was discussed in chapter 5, we spent a lot of time in 2009 and 2010 building lending and 401(k) rollover relationships and have the tools and contacts available as part of our sales process. We were also successful in 2010 in securing a credit facility that provides SBA loans according to preestablished criteria.

Preparing a pro-forma income statement and cash flow statement is part of a prospect's responsibility at the conclusion of step 2. We provide a blank template with the row headings that correspond with the disclosures in the FDD to assist a prospect in preparing a pro-forma as a component of accessing financing. Also at the end of step 2, the prospect gains access to our FDD, which contains a robust Item 19 regarding historical financial performance results, as well as the cost (of initial and ongoing investments) assumptions and many of the revenue and cost-of-goods-sold assumptions based on what our franchisees have experienced. We want her to prepare her assumptions for this pro-forma so she can ask franchisees questions to validate those assumptions. We are very clear and strict in telling all prospects that we are unable to discuss or review their pro-forma. Be sure to tell every prospect this; potential legal issues could arise otherwise. As I have mentioned earlier, the franchise laws regulate the offer and sales process. It is important for you to understand what you can do during the process and what actions or statements can get you into legal trouble. This is particularly true if you do not provide a detailed Item 19 in your FDD.

The prospect is given access to download our FDD and to listen to an audio presentation covering the highlights of the FDD, the franchise agreement, and the area development agreement. At this point we also need to know if there are any areas that the prospect sees as "deal killers," so that we can work through them. This doesn't mean we negotiate and modify our franchise agreement, because we don't, but getting our director of contract administration or our attorney on the phone to explain the intention of a particular section often can move us forward. You will need to evaluate the appropriate stage in your process to deliver the FDD, especially if you do not have an Item 19 financial performance representation.

Lastly, we grant access to a weekly senior leadership call hosted by either our president or me. We introduce this at the end of step 2 to better inform the prospect about the highlights of the system and our strategic priorities. The call format is one hour, 40 minutes of which is devoted to a PowerPoint presentation and the remaining time to open questions.

STEP THREE: TRAINING AND SUPPORT

The Training and Support section is an in-depth review of the resources we provide to franchisees from (1) signing to opening, (2) immediately following opening, and (3) then on an ongoing basis. Some concepts may also incorporate site visits to allow the prospect to experience firsthand a day in the life of a franchisee. This step may be helpful if a prospect needs it to alleviate fear, but it can create issues because it may introduce a lot of variables that you cannot control.

At this stage, we invite the prospect and any spouse or partner that will be actively involved in the business to complete an online profile assessment. The profile assessment that we use looks at values, motives, leadership style, and competencies. We have moved this up earlier in the process, from step 5 to step 3, so that we can focus our sales team on working with prospects who could ultimately be the right fit for us and where we can be the right fit for them. We have developed a "top performer" profile by reviewing our top performing franchisees and surveying them to find common characteristics. Using these tools improves our odds of having high-performing franchisees.

Step Four: Validation

Step 4 in our process is Validation. Providing access for a prospect to talk to franchisees is an important part of the process through which the prospect can validate what she heard during the sales process. Our validation actually begins at the end of step 3 with an invitation to attend weekly franchisee-hosted group validation calls. On advice from our attorneys, we do not attend these hosted validation calls, nor do we handpick only top performers to host the calls, as the host may be at any level within the bell-shaped curve of performance in the system. As in every other aspect of your franchise sales process, make sure you understand the legal aspects of validation, as there are practices that are acceptable and other practices that can be problematic. For example, a franchisor who does not include any financial performance information in Item 19 of its FDD and steers candidates only to its top performers as part of validation not only may have legal issues but also is creating a situation in which the candidate may not have a realistic expectation of the franchise opportunity.

Our purpose for the validation step is to provide candidates with additional perspective of what BrightStar is all about—the good and the not so good. It is important to not stage or improperly influence the process. We emphasize access to information so that a candidate can make an informed decision on whether we might be the right fit for what she is seeking in a franchise opportunity.

It is absolutely critical in the validation process that the salesperson never set up an expectation of Utopia in what the prospect will hear. Rather, the salesperson explains for the prospect what the key performance indicators are for the system (for us, that may be sales call activity, dollars spent on advertising and recruiting, recruiting activity, call conversion, and net promoter score). The prospect should then be encouraged to ask how the franchisee is performing on these key performance indicators. Ultimately, the prospect wants to learn what to replicate from strong performers, what to avoid from weak performers, and what the franchisees she encounters would do again or would have done differently. This helps to frame the feedback and also provides valuable information for the prospect, if she becomes a franchisee, to focus on the right things to improve results.

We have also worked with our attorneys to provide, through our sales process, some suggested questions that a candidate may want to consider asking our franchisees as part of the validation step and some key tips in terms of being respectful of a franchisee's time. (We advise the prospect that if she joins the BrightStar system she may be receiving these calls in the future.) Of course, the candidate is free to ask whatever questions she wants. We just want to make sure she is asking some of the critical questions, so that she can better understand the BrightStar business she is considering. We also spend time educating our franchisees on the important role they play in validation and thanking them for taking the time to help prospects decide if we are the right opportunity for them and helping us decide if the prospect is right for us. We encourage our franchisees to provide feedback to the sales team if they have questions about the fit of a prospect. A word of caution is necessary in this regard: Ensure that a franchisee's negative feedback about a given prospect isn't proffered because the franchisee doesn't want a neighboring territory sold that he himself may be selling into. On the other hand, if the complaint is related to a market halfway across the country, it probably should be taken very seriously.

STEP FIVE: JOIN-THE-TEAM DAY

The final step includes checking all the remaining boxes to ensure that the prospect is ready to attend our Join-the-Team Day (JTTD) and then does, indeed, attend. If the prospect indicates at any point during the sales process that she will have an attorney review the documents, encourage her to have that done prior to Join-the-Team Day; don't delay this step until after that celebratory event (franchisees will never be as high emotionally prior to joining the family as they are on Join-the-Team Day). We do not discourage prospects from consulting with a lawyer as part of their due diligence. In fact, if they do, we like to see a prospect use an attorney with franchise experience.

As part of our final set of steps to ensure that a prospect is ready for JTTD, we process a background and credit check. A prospect must have a clean background check because our business entails taking care of families. We also want to ensure that the prospect has a high enough credit score to obtain financing. This is a critical step and only because of the cost do we wait until near the end of the process. That said, as part of the access to financing review, we do make it clear that a minimum credit score of 685 is needed to participate in our credit facility.

Once we verify acceptable background and credit checks, the prospect is scheduled for an interview with our brand president to ensure that the prospect fits our values, is willing to put in the effort to succeed, is able to follow the model, and has the experience and attitude we seek. On this call the brand president approves or denies each prospect to attend JTTD and discusses the profile results with the prospect so the prospect knows where she fits well and what areas will need to be focused on. Occasionally, a prospect with a successful corporate track record but poorly matched profile result is *conditionally* approved for JTTD to give us an opportunity to evaluate the prospect in person and to consider having the prospect retake the profile. (As we will discuss in the next chapter, a profile test can sometimes have inaccurate results if a candidate is experiencing significant trauma and/or change in her life.) If a prospect is denied for attending JTTD, the brand president goes back to the salesperson to coach him or her as to why the candidate is not approved to move forward.

Our JTTD begins on a Thursday evening, when two or three of our senior leadership team members have dinner with all of the prospects. We particularly enjoy this social time over dinner to get to know one another better and to observe how the prospects interact with one another and with the wait staff. Franchisees will need to inspire a diverse workforce, and we need to see that they appreciate all people, not just those in a suit and tie. It is also amazing what you hear when folks drop their guard. On a few occasions I've had a private conversation with a prospect following dinner and offered to pay travel costs (which we do not do otherwise) because during dinner it became clear that the prospect was not the right fit for BrightStar. These are delicate situations, but they reinforce with the group the next day at our home offices that we really "select" our franchisees rather than "sell" franchises.

We spend about seven hours on Friday with a combination of presentation/Q&A sessions and individual rotations with key team members. We limit attendance to no more than six prospects (if each brought a spouse that could be a total of 12 people) so that we have ample time to get to know one another. We meet as a leadership team afterward and approve or deny by committee, and then our head of franchise sales informs the sales team of the results and the prospects are notified. We ask for a decision from an approved prospect within one week of granting approval; she is told that the territory is available for sale to others until she signs a franchise agreement. Unless there are extraordinary circumstances, after one week we close out a prospect who has not signed a franchise agreement. For those who do sign our franchise agreement, we have our preopening concierge make contact the same day and begin orienting them as to the resources available and scheduling them for training.

You will hear most franchisors refer to their final step in the process as "Discovery Day." We changed the name from Discovery Day, which is a common term in franchising, to Join-the-Team Day, to ensure that we were setting the right expectations for this step in the process. Some franchisors use the visit as an opportunity to share key information to help prospects decide whether or not to move forward in the process. For our Join-the-Team Day, however, we set the expectation that there is nothing to "discover" but rather an opportunity to validate what they have heard. We see the JTTD as a mutual opportunity to assess our values and culture "fit."

Sales Personnel

A great sales process guides good prospects through to the point of joining the system while it simultaneously weeds out those incapable of following a process and identifies those who are simply not a good fit for us, and vice versa. The highest cost of the franchise sales process isn't the money to get the leads; rather, it's the compensation of your personnel. Be sure you set up your technology and design your process in a way that ensures that your salespeople spend their time with the right prospects.

Number of Sales Personnel Needed

It is necessary to define how many prospects a salesperson can effectively handle. Generally, 25 to 35 active prospects (i.e., qualified leads with CQ) in the pipeline would be the right volume, regardless of the salesperson's skill level and capacity. Each prospect typically should be given about an hour of attention per week during your process (generally, the process is five to seven weeks), and you'll hope to have five to 10 new prospects weekly that will each need an introductory call. If you have a sales team of more than one salesperson and each salesperson has fewer than 25 active prospects, then you need to either increase leads or consider a reduction in the team. Conversely, if all of your salespeople are each handling close to 35 active qualified leads, then it is time to consider adding another salesperson to the team, because 35 active qualified leads represents about a 50-hour workweek and that is about as much as any salesperson can effectively handle.

Each salesperson hired must understand that she is expected to work nights and weekends, when people are free to have relaxed and confidential conversations about what they want their lives to look like. Night and weekend calls are also important to ensure that both spouses or partners are engaged in the process. Working only with the husband or wife for weeks and then expecting the spouse or partner to buy in from only attending JTTD is unrealistic.

Outsourcing Sales

It is becoming more common for start-up franchisors to outsource their franchise sales function. Companies such as Franchise Performance Group, Kiekenapp and Associates, and Brand One have a solid reputation for getting deals done. Hiring them can be a good option for adding franchisees, especially because such companies normally charge a flat fee or a percentage of the franchise fee when a deal closes, so you only pay out of the money collected from your new franchisee and you don't have fixed overhead costs.

We have used an outsourced option for a portion of our deals when we needed additional sales support but didn't quite need another full-time salesperson. We successfully negotiated the contract to allow us, for a set fee, to bring the consultant on as an employee. Four months into the contract we triggered this clause and hired this individual as the third salesperson on our team.

We never chose to outsource all franchise sales. Although to do so would have conserved cash flow in the first year or two, we wanted to develop a culture based on selecting the right franchisees ourselves. The very real possibility that the relationship with one of these outsourced groups would become strained concerned me, for if we turned down a prospect they sent to participate in Join-the-Team Day they would not get a fee. My employees get a base salary to screen and filter prospects, and we share in the success of selecting the right franchisee through awarding a franchise—franchise fees for the company and commissions for our salespeople.

That said, and depending on your capitalization level when you launch your franchise system, outsourcing your sales team could be a viable option for you to consider. Screen companies to determine whether they are aligned with you as to the qualities you are seeking in a franchisee. Ensure that the outsource group is committed to approving only franchisees that meet your criteria. Insist on interviewing the franchisee recruiter (franchise salesperson) running point on your account. If you wouldn't hire that person if given the chance, if he isn't a fit for your company, and if you wouldn't personally make an investment in him if you were the prospect, take a pass.

A word of caution in the way you structure compensation for an outsourced sales resource (or in how you will compensate franchise brokers, discussed in detail in chapter 7): some outsourced sales resources and/or franchise brokers will attempt to negotiate for a percentage of your ongoing royalty that you will receive from a franchisee that they helped to place with you, for a fixed period of time or in perpetuity. I strongly advise against ever giving away a portion of your royalties. You do not know yet what your cost of supporting the franchisee will be, and an agreement like this may leave you with inadequate net royalties to provide the proper level of support. Negotiate a fixed amount for each franchisee you approve or a variable percentage of the amount of initial franchise fees you collect.

Benefits of a Sales Qualifier

Hiring a sales qualifier was one of our best investments. Notice I used the term *investment*, not *cost*.

BRIGHT IDEA:

The use of a great sales qualifier adds to our ability to increase deals and to maximize our sales team's time.

Our sales qualifier makes a great first impression and allows us to be available when a prospect calls in. Most prospects communicate online, but the phone number is on the website and occasionally we receive calls. Since the sales team are on the phone all day, having a sales qualifier available to take an inbound call creates a better experience than having the call go to voicemail.

We wanted someone with a high level of passion and energy, and our sales qualifier has that. In fact, our sales qualifier is so good that BrightStar took the first place Star Award for Best Telephone Prospect Follow-Up at the 2010 Franchise Update Media Group's Leadership & Development Conference. In addition to the first impression she makes, our energetic and impassioned sales qualifier provides some initial information to the prospect while assessing the prospect's fit by extracting the following information: (1) the financial match to our investment level and net worth criteria; (2) the timing match for making a decision within the next three months; (3) the geography match for territory we have available with a willingness on their part to consider alternatives; and (4) the skills-and-experience match. Any prospect that does not meet our first three matches is ruled out. When a prospect aligns on the first three, our sales qualifier delivers the information the salesperson needs about the prospect's background, skills, and experience and schedules a call between the prospect and the salesperson.

We took an unconventional route in filling the sales qualifier position by looking for an employee's spouse who could work from home. As we grow, we will look to this type of source again. Our employees are passionate about BrightStar, and they discuss with their families the story we are writing together. What better way to keep the family involved than to have the husband and wife both working at BrightStar? While you have to ensure that spouses are in different roles and not reporting to one another, we have had great success with couples in our workplace.

Key Franchise Sales Metrics

Being a CPA, I tend to watch the numbers—particularly key metrics—probably more than most CEOs. Numbers don't intrigue everyone equally, but before you doze off, make a note to yourself to discuss this section with your numbers person and your head of franchise sales. It's important that the three of you are watching and measuring the same things.

Though many companies watch the metrics discussed here, I am surprised by how many do not. It's evident from the responses to industry surveys that a fairly significant percentage of companies do not know their cost per sale or their cost per lead or the sources of their deals. By knowing what metrics to watch, what goals to set for your team, and how to prioritize your efforts (the topics covered in the following sections), you will be well prepared to ensure that you optimize your efficiency and maximize your organization's ROI for your franchise sales activity.

Setting Goals for Spending and Deals

To set goals, it is critical to understand the relationship between what you spend on lead generation, what lead sources you use, and the skills of the sales team to achieve higher close rates (defined below) and the number of new franchisees you are likely to be able to add. I am often surprised that some franchisors do not connect these dots and do not leverage as many lead sources as possible to improve results. To illustrate the interrelationship, let me share a conversation that I frequently have at franchise industry networking events. When I am talking with a franchise sales manager, and she says that her company doesn't use brokers (third-party lead sources that identify, qualify, and introduce prospects to your concept, discussed more fully in chapter 7), I ask her how many new franchisees they plan to add in the following year. When she says 30, I then ask what their lead generation budget is, and she says it was cut to $100,000. Those numbers imply that this company hopes to achieve a cost per completion of a little more than $3,000 (calculated by using the $100,000 budget divided by the 30 expected new deals for the budget to generate).

Industry surveys and my own recent experience put the cost per completion, for most concepts with an investment above $50,000, in the $7,000 to $9,000 range. The franchise sales manager's company already has the cards stacked against it. Based on these more accurate ($7,000 to $9,000) numbers, the company will need a budget of $210,000 to $270,000 to close 30 new franchisees. Moreover, if they've targeted 30 deals and have a one percent close rate (which is really good, and means that one out of 100 of the suspects that look at your brand buy your franchise), they would need at least 3,000 leads. With an average cost per suspect of $50 to $70, they would need a budget of $150,000 to $210,000—and that is only if they can maintain an overall close rate of 1 percent of all non-broker suspects. A 1 percent close rate would be very high for portals (Internet-based lead generation sites; see chapter 7). This means that the franchise sales manager had better know her numbers (the cost per close, the cost per suspect, and the close rate, which varies by concept and their investment range) and industry information to benchmark before signing off on goals, because the number of deals and the budget to get them must be linked.

I recommend that your senior leadership team (most important, the CEO, the CFO, and the head of franchise sales) be aligned on the answers to the following questions and understand that the answers complement one another: (1) What is my franchise sales lead generation budget? (2) How many franchisees should that budget produce? (3) How many new franchisees are budgeted? and (4) Where will my deals be coming from? That is, what percentage will come from brokers (not included in question 1, but should be budgeted in the financials—usually as a separate account called "broker fees") and what percentage will come from non-brokers?

The real issue arises when questions 2 and 3 fall out of alignment because the franchise sales lead generation budget is inadequate to produce the results required.

Let's look at a common situation in which this can occur:

+ Franchise sales lead generation budget: $200,000
+ Assumptions: one-half (0.5) percent close rate on non-broker leads and cost per suspect is $50
+ CEO signs off on adding 40 new franchisees, 30 of which will be from non-broker sources and 10 will be from brokers.

The answer to question 1 above is $200,000. Using a 0.5 percent close rate to answer question 2, we need 6,000 leads (calculated using the 30 non-broker deals divided by the 0.5 percent close rate) to achieve 30 non-broker completions, and at $50 per suspect, the budget needed is $300,000 (calculated by multiplying the 6,000 suspects needed by the $50 cost per suspect). The budget of $200,000 will produce only 20 non-broker deals (calculated by dividing the $200,000 by $50 to determine the number of suspects that budget can generate, or 4,000 suspects, and then multiplying this by the 0.005 close rate). The answer to question 3, however, is that the CEO is expecting 30 non-broker deals and 10 broker deals for a total of 40 new franchisees. So 2 and 3 are out of alignment.

To resolve the discrepancy, either the non-broker goal needs to be reduced to 20 or the available lead generation budget needs to be increased. Likewise, the percentage of deals coming through brokers may need to be increased to achieve the goals, and new strategies may need to be developed to increase the number of broker deals. This could be a long shot, depending on past broker results, and this will impact the net deal income (franchise fees received less broker fees paid out) and the expectations that will need to be discussed.

I also recommend that your head of operations be consulted on the number of new franchisees planned for the year. This will assure you that the infrastructure is already in place, or that the company has planned for additional resources, to support the new franchisees while honoring commitments to your existing franchisees.

You may now be asking how you can determine the number of suspects you need. You can make some assumptions based on the number of non-broker deals you plan to close and conservatively assume you will need to generate 200 suspects (a 0.5 percent suspect-to-completion ratio) for every deal you want to close. Some systems are very successful with website leads, referrals, and public relations and therefore skew their suspect-to-completion ratio to 1 percent or 2 percent to offset the lower percentage that portals normally achieve. It is better to plan conservatively than to (1) wind up with idle salespeople who do not have enough suspects to have 25 to 35 active leads (CQ qualified) in their pipeline consistently; (2) fail to meet your growth goals that were communicated to your bank; or (3) fail to leverage the infrastructure put in place ahead of the planned growth.

Evaluating the Cost to Generate Leads

Most discussions about this topic focus only on two data points: the cost per suspect, which the industry refers to as the "cost per lead," and the cost per completion, which the industry refers to as the "cost per sale." For me, it's important to evaluate lead sources and their ROI based on the following calculations:

+ Cost per suspect (or industry denoted "cost per lead")
+ Cost per CQ (or qualified lead)
+ Cost per completion (or closed sale)

Cost per suspect is a metric to assess the return on producing a certain quantity of suspects. For portals that cost a similar flat fee per month, the cost per suspect is better based on a higher quantity of suspects. The more meaningful review comes from knowing what sources are producing the highest quality leads. Cost per CQ allows you to evaluate lead-source quality that can be masked by a poor cost per completion because cost per completion factors in the salesperson's ability *and* the quality of the lead.

For example, one source from which we get an average of 35 suspects monthly costs $30 per suspect. A little less than 5 percent of them convert from a suspect to a CQ, so the cost per CQ is approximately $600 (calculated by dividing the $30 by 0.05) and the cost per completion is approximately $6,400. It took 427 suspects to get merely two completions (slightly lower than a 0.5 percent suspect-to-completion ratio), but for us this is an acceptable cost per completion. (I have coached franchisors who have cancelled contracts because they considered 427 suspects to get two completions to be ineffective and they did not know their cost per completion before making the decision.) This is why it is important to know your numbers and be able to evaluate each lead source.

You may wonder how hard it is to do this type of review and how often you should do it. It took me less than five minutes to review the previous example. Most of the inputs were easily displayed within Process Peak on one screen, and the system allows me to review the inputs by lead source in seconds each. (This is another example of how technology can work for you.) Build the discipline to perform this analysis per lead source prior to renewing a contract to see if the contract should be renewed or allowed to cancel, or if the amount allocated for spending should actually be increased. For sources that are perpetual, such as pay-per-click, this analysis should be done monthly. I recommend reviewing the year-to-date information and analyzing the month-to-month trend, because looking at the information in a one-month vacuum can be misleading.

We see our cost per suspect ranging from $30 to $150, depending on which portal or pay-per-click method they are coming from. Our cost per CQ ranges from $90 to $900. Our cost per close has increased from $7,000 in 2008 to $9,000 in 2009; it was back down to about $8,500 in 2010. I make decisions on what to renew, what to cancel, and where to allocate more dollars based upon the cost per completion and cost per CQ because those are ROI measurements based upon lead quality—generating a lot of leads, and having a low-cost per suspect, is a measurement of quantity, not quality and not ROI.

Evaluating Salespeople

Every industry is different, and the size of the investment will impact the number of deals a company may be able to close in a given year. Also, whether a salesperson is handling broker or Internet leads will significantly impact his ratios. Given that a completed confidential questionnaire amounts to a tentative commitment, I have found that once we look at the ratios of CQs to completed deals, there is no material correlation with the source of the suspect (broker or Internet). There *is* a significant disparity in the *suspect*-to-completion ratios because Internet suspects are generally far less qualified than broker suspects; broker leads have been contacted and have been prequalified as a potential fit. Many Internet leads will not even respond to phone or e-mail contact.

When evaluating salespeople, it is typical to focus on the number of deals closed. I agree that this is important, but I care even more about what their CQ-to-completed-deal ratio is because that shows me how many more deals we could close if we increased the ratios of our weaker salespeople to average or to high-level performance ratios. (We bring the team together three or four times per year and invest in sharing best practices, role playing, and bringing in third parties—such as Sandler Sales Training—who can help our sales staff improve skills to achieve higher completion ratios.)

The salesperson's CQ-to-completed-deal ratio also highlights whether I need to make changes in the department. The last thing you want is to have a salesperson on your staff who is unable to maximize the potential of moving a qualified lead to completion.

Ensuring the highest completion ratios is important in terms of profitability when it comes to non-broker completions, but it can have an even greater impact for broker completions. Franchisors with a reputation for high completion ratios get more broker leads—it is just a fact. Brokers want to place prospects with the right concept for a good match, but they also need to place them where the deal will get closed. Otherwise, the broker will not earn a commission.

Certainly completion ratios vary by industry and by salesperson, but I've found that looking at completion ratios is the best way to factor out the impact of a recession. Suspects are certainly down for most companies and most industries, but generally the completion ratios are not that different. The broker networks look for a close ratio of 10 percent. Though I would love to achieve that ratio consistently across my team, I look for an 8 to 10 percent close ratio on broker leads (the CQ-to-completion ratio is similar for non-broker leads too). I look for a base level of performance for new salespeople of at least a 5 percent close ratio on broker leads and at least 12 to 15 completions in their first year (based upon driving a minimum of 300 CQ's per salesperson per year). As a salesperson's performance increases to 18 to 22 completions per year, her base compensation increases by nearly 50 percent. A salesperson with annual completions at or above 24 has a base salary double that of the salesperson with 12 to 15 annual completions. In a results-oriented culture, we reward performance both in commission (each deal receives a commission) and in terms of base pay and the number of stock options for our high performers.

Evaluating the Process

Another way to consistently improve performance is to evaluate your process monthly. Each month we spend time with our representative from Process Peak to review his insights and, in particular, to evaluate any changes in the progression of candidates from one stage to the next. As an example, you may see attrition among those expected to move from the validation stage (in which they get feedback from current franchisees) to the Join-the-Team-Day stage, which can be an early indication that your franchisees are not validating well. For a variety of reasons, this would be valuable to know immediately so you can improve franchisee satisfaction without waiting until your next franchisee survey and so you don't lose potential deals due to poor validation.

In addition, you need to know the trend of the conversion ratios overall by suspect-to-CQ, CQ-to-completion, and suspect-to-completion. This information will signal changes that may need to be investigated. High-level ratios, when compared to the year-to-date numbers in the prior month, can indicate that a lead source has fallen off in quantity or quality or both, or that a particular salesperson's numbers are down.

In my opinion, every CEO should receive reporting from the head of franchise sales on the above numbers and be able to explain any negative change and come up with an action plan to address it. At one time I delegated all reporting to my head of franchise sales, but after seeing early warning indicators and digging in, I realized that we had lost nearly six months on Internet lead flow from a change in our website that no one had caught, and we had lost nearly a year on broker lead flow. I then mandated the review of these key statistics, so now our senior leadership team reviews the statistics weekly (to varying degrees in a one-hour meeting) and monthly (as part of a five-hour meeting). I now am comfortable knowing that everyone is looking at and owning the numbers. If they're not, at least I won't lose more than 30 days in discovering it and ensuring that an action plan is in place to address it.

Closing Thoughts

A sales process is the key to optimizing results and scaling in the number of new franchisees added. We reviewed technology and processes to assist you with designing an effective sales process from day one. Keep in mind that a defined sales process that fits you and your system will enable you to simultaneously evaluate whether a prospect is right for you while the prospect decides whether your concept is right for him. That prospect's positive decision depends on how forthright and organized you are in delivering pertinent information to and for him. In addition, you have learned the most critical metrics to watch to ensure, as we dive into the sources of generating suspects in the next chapter, that you will spend your money wisely and know what levers to pull to get a different result. No sales process is perfect. Not every franchisee who joins the system will succeed, but a good sales process will improve the likelihood that you and your candidates will decide that the fit is right to move forward with the opportunity.

· · ·

Now that you have a handle on the sales process, let's create a plan to generate leads so you can maximize your results.

CHAPTER 7

Lead Generation: Finding the

Right Franchisees

The two main ideas in this chapter work hand in hand: (1) defining the profile of your ideal franchisee, and (2) finding the ideal franchisee who is looking for your type of opportunity. It's obviously more cost-effective to define who you are looking for first, before you spend money trying to generate leads.

Whom Are You Looking For?

Defining the profile of the ideal franchisee is one of the most important tasks for a franchisor to perform. It is important that the people you want also want you. Make sure that your ideal prospect aligns with what such a prospect would be seeking in terms of financial rewards, quality-of-life returns, and the day-to-day responsibilities. For example, we want a franchisee to be actively engaged, competitive and driven to build a business, and have the heart and personal experience to also be in the business for the right reasons. We therefore seek and attract those who want to build a scalable business, want to make a difference, and are willing to work a lot of hours early on to establish and grow the business.

The kind of people you want and who want an opportunity like yours directly impacts the lead-generation strategies you will implement, but it also should influence the design of your sales process. Effective lead generation is about attracting high-quality prospects that match what you are seeking in a franchisee. Some prospects want more information—such as understanding a day in the life of a franchisee, client and caregiver stories, and key performance indicators (data) of the business—and some want only the key bullet points and choose to drill into areas important to them. Throughout this chapter you will learn more about ensuring that your sales team factors candidate profiles into their sales process.

As important as it is to identify promising prospects, you still have to be selective regarding which prospects—even apparently ideal ones—to "sell." For example, although there are always exceptions, I recommend against selling franchises to friends or family or to the children of friends. I am similarly cautious about parents buying their child a business, because an owner-operator needs skin in the game. BrightStar supports parent-child franchisees on an exception basis where the parent commits to being actively involved day-to-day in developing her adult child's management skills and overseeing and leading the business.

I recommend that your senior leadership team spend time to develop the profile of your ideal franchisee. The profile should include such details as the ideal gender, age or age range, whether he needs management or industry experience, if he needs certain educational or experience levels, and what level of capitalization and liquidity he needs. If you are having difficulty in the very beginning in defining the profile of a franchisee, start by recruiting franchisees who are similar to the founder.

It may be difficult to determine the exact traits for an ideal profile before you have franchisees, but giving it some thought early on better prepares you for your search. As you grow your base of franchisees, commit to reviewing their profiles annually to evaluate if there are common traits among your top performers, such as education, experience level, background (sales or operations), energy level, positive attitude, etc., and begin using this information to refine your profile. At BrightStar, we see that over 80 percent of our franchisees have a college education and over 10 years of employment experience and that our top performers generally managed large teams of employees and had profit-and-loss accountability.

I am a big believer in using technology-based profiling tools to help gather information on all prospects who will join our system. You may not be able to establish patterns until you have 20 or 25 franchisees in your system. You can still draft a profile in the interim, consistent with the roles and responsibilities of the franchisees in the business as a starting point and with character qualities consistent with the culture.

We have used three profiling companies, and there are many more to choose from. We initially selected a tool that was inexpensive and easy to execute but found no correlation between what the test predicted and the actual results. We moved to a second tool that was much more predictive of success in terms of revenue performance, but it did not help us ensure that owners were a culture fit.

The profiling company we chose in 2010 has provided us with a competitive advantage in the selection of franchisees. Most profile tools merely assess personality or work style, but our new vendor, Proven Match, actually includes seven assessments in one comprehensive test that measures values and motives, emotional and social intelligence, core competencies, work style, stage of growth, focus preference, and leadership. Because work style (what is generally the only component measured by other profile tools) is only 10 percent of the overall measure of compatibility and performance, Proven Match puts a much greater emphasis on values and motives, emotional and social intelligence, and core competencies.

In addition to using the profiles to identify who we are seeking, we have also identified certain components that are common to poor performers and missing from top performers. The earlier we spot them, the better it is for the suspect and for us, because we don't spend weeks of each other's time before rejecting the prospect as a franchisee. As an example, we have determined that franchisees whose profiles show low levels of self-awareness of their weaknesses will generally perform poorly in our system. Their lack of self-awareness makes them less willing to receive feedback, actively seek learning and experience to overcome weaknesses, or hire to mitigate these limitations. Likewise, a profile that indicates that a prospect will be unlikely to lead through directing (but instead makes most decisions by group consensus) will likely struggle, because her employees and referral sources won't trust her to have a vision of the business and be capable of driving it.

I recommend that you work with a profiling company that charges per test (usually negotiable to between $20 and $30 per test) so that you don't have to commit to large fixed amounts too early before you determine the quality of the information and the correlation of the profile to performance.

BRIGHT IDEA:

Ask your chosen profiling company to build a "top performer" model by surveying your top-performing franchisees to find consistent traits, so that you can begin selecting franchisees more likely to become top performers.

Every two years (ideally this will become annually) I survey the franchise system, or as many franchisees as will respond, to clearly understand the profile of the ideal franchisee—the top performers. This is important for systems that have rapid growth, high levels of system change, and/or large investments in innovation that require franchisee adoption (and an ability to effectively manage change) because the ideal profile will change during these phases of franchisor transformation. Along with establishing what you will look for in new franchisees, this system-wide approach also helps you understand the makeup of your system and the patterns of beliefs, preferences, values, etc., among all levels of performers. Even though it's difficult to determine whether middle performers will become high performers if you can ignite more passion in them, it is worth the investment to work with them to improve their performance. On the other hand, bottom performers can mean the death of a good franchise system because they drain resources and will emotionally wear out your support team.

I like to augment my review of these profile assessments by looking at a correlation between a few internal metrics and profile types. The metrics may vary by system, but spending the time to evaluate multiple internal factors to grade a franchisee's fit—in correlation with his profile type— is a valuable exercise. Using this approach would have helped us greatly had we identified the distinctions earlier in our history. The review process includes the following steps:

1. Based on revenue performance from opening to current date compared to the system goal for her first unit only, categorize each franchisee according to her first unit performance: T for top performers (top 25 percent), M for average performers (middle 50 percent), or B for bottom performers (bottom 25 percent). This will assess her performance as a single-unit owner-operator.

2. Based on revenue performance from opening to current date compared to the system goal for the aggregate of all units, categorize each franchisee according to her total business performance. (Use the T, M, or B categories described in item 1.) This will assess her performance as a multi-unit operator. Some franchisees will show that they underperform as a multi-unit operator because they lack leadership skills and/or have a tendency to micromanage, but they may be solid

single-unit performers. Addressing the need to develop new skills or to sell off a territory can be a win-win way to improve the franchisee's ROI.

3. Identify franchisees who are costly to support and/or do not value the franchise relationship.
4. Identify the role the franchisee started in (operations or sales); what role she is in now (operations or sales); if she changed roles, and if so, how long it took; and, if she had to do it again knowing what she knows now, what role she would have started in. The roles may be different for your system, but usually there is a core role or two that a franchisee can choose. It's also possible that a given franchisee began as an investor (which we do not allow in our system) without involvement and then became an owner-operator or, conversely, began as an owner-operator and then moved out of the day-to-day to an investor role.

Your operations department should be able to complete items 1, 2, and 3. Item 4 will require involving your franchisees to help gather the information. Use these data in evaluating the ideal franchisee profile. It will also be valuable when we get to chapter 8 and look at how franchisors make their money.

In addition to learning that a multi-unit operator had a different profile from a single-unit operator, we learned that we had to update our ideal franchisee profile for changes in how he accessed capital and when our model required new skills.

In mid-2009 we changed our model from one in which the franchisee had to perform the outside sales function to one in which our franchisee could perform the operations role and hire an outside salesperson. We actually saw improved performance when our franchisees were in the operations role, and we saw that the transition from single-unit to multi-unit leadership was easier when the franchisee had started in the operations role. We had adapted the model so much that we were probably looking for an operations and leadership generalist instead of a salesperson. It took us between 12 and 18 months to identify that our profile needed to change to reflect this, and we needed to resurvey our franchisees to gather the information necessary to establish a new ideal franchisee profile.

AVOID THIS PITFALL:

By evaluating franchisees annually to see if the ideal (top performer) profile in a prior year is still relevant today, you mitigate your risk of not maximizing a solid tool.

Refer to the profile of your ideal franchisee to assist you in evaluating where this type of individual will listen, watch, or read to learn about (franchise) opportunities. You will use this valuable information as you negotiate with lead-generation sources to ensure that where (i.e., portals, print, radio, cable, etc.) you spend money to advertise targets the demographic profile of your ideal franchisee. The profile will also assist you in developing messages for the various marketing initiatives.

Customary Lead Sources

Now that you have a solid sales process and know the profile of the ideal franchisee that you are looking for, it is time to understand the various sources of leads. You will be in control of your visibility through your own website and through your public relations (PR) strategy. In addition, there are sources dedicated to cultivating franchise leads for you through portals and print advertising. You pay for these services without knowing if they will be successful or not. Broker networks are also available to assist you in identifying prospects that may be good franchisee candidates. You pay brokers when and if you award their prospect a franchise.

Franchise Website

I am always amazed when I hear about the huge sums franchisors spend generating leads and then look at their website and find it unappealing or difficult to navigate. Why spend money to get a suspect to your website and then create a poor experience, making them "bounce" off the site and not provide any contact information for your franchise salesperson to follow up on?

Here are a couple of thoughts about designing an effective franchise website based on my own experience: (1) Separate your customer website from your franchise website; (2) pick a web designer knowledgeable about franchising; (3) design your website to direct the prospect through a specific process to learn about your concept; and (4) select a web designer who understands search engine optimization so that your website is not just pretty but also attracts leads. I would also recommend a place on the homepage where the content is regularly changed and updated (i.e., company news, message from the CEO, etc.).

Customers are seeking different information from what a franchise prospect is looking for, and you want the primary function of your customer site to build brand awareness and influence a purchase to increase the revenues for your franchisees. You want to lead prospects directly to your franchise site so you can watch the analytics to see where leads are coming from. Being in home care and taking seriously the part we play in families' lives, BrightStar didn't want to send the wrong message, that we can care for your parent or child and also sell you a franchise. For a while, then, we didn't even have a way to get to our franchise site from our customer site. But eventually we added a link as a secondary component in our customer page design. For any other industry, I would display it more prominently because we've come to realize that the number one source of leads on our franchise site comes from our customer site. Think of your franchise site as the executive summary of a business plan and the new "gatekeeper" of what the business is and isn't.

Market Awareness

I am a big believer in public relations regardless of the size of your system. We generate at least one or two sales per year with prospects who found us because of an article or a TV appearance. Those two sales alone give us a positive return on our annual PR investment. I also believe there is much more indirect benefit from PR because customers and prospects become aware of the brand and then visit the website.

It may be best to delay a PR effort until you have between five and 10 franchisees, so that you have something to pitch. Prior to that point, you may not have a solid return on those precious funds.

Advertising

Advertising is another method to generate awareness and visibility, and ultimately prospects. As a place to start, you will want to look into the various venues where your competitors or similar investment-range concepts are advertising. The number of advertising choices you make will largely be determined by your lead-generation budget. Once you begin advertising, use the metrics discussed in chapter 6 to determine which lead sources produce the best results.

Internet Portals

An Internet portal is a website that spends money on search engine marketing (SEM) and search engine optimization (SEO) to attract potential franchisees to the site to look at various franchise concepts in exchange for completing a short profile with an e-mail address. The site, or "portal," then sends these profiles to various franchisors that have paid to advertise and paid to receive leads. There is a vast number of portal choices to advertise on. Many franchisors are willing to share information about which portals are working well for them, if you ask. You just need to make sure the portals are appropriate for your organization.

AVOID THIS PITFALL:

One of the biggest mistakes I made early on was assuming that all portals that other franchisors were using successfully would work for me too.

I collected portal references from sales gurus I respected, and after signing year-long contracts, discovered that the portal that worked for them didn't work so well for us. I spent a fortune generating only a handful of qualified leads before it dawned on me that I require an owner-operator, and most often the sales gurus I consulted with sold mostly investor-model franchise concepts that appeal to executives who want to keep their jobs.

I share this painful discovery because it is critical to gather information based on matching a few key parameters: (1) owner-operator or investor model; (2) investment range—under $50K, $50K–$100K, $100K–$250K, and above $250K; (3) sector (food, retail, or service); and (4) home-based or not. The quality of leads varies by sites: Some are just awful for all concepts, some are good for some concepts but not others, and a few sites are good overall. But how can you judge if a portal is good?

I spend time on evaluating lead quality on portals because it is more important to have a reasonable cost per completion (closed deal) than it is to have a low cost per suspect. For instance, if the suspects answer my e-mail or take my call and then enough of them buy so that my cost per completion is less than $9,000, I judge those leads to be quality leads. Certain sites do not generate much quantity for my company, but the lead quality is high.

In selecting portals to start with, I recommend the following steps to improve your odds of success and positive ROI:

1. See what comes up on a Google search of "franchise opportunity" and make a list of all franchise portal advertisements. The higher the

ranking in the Google list, the better the portal's SEO and likely the better the lead flow through the site. Click on the link to each site, find the information for advertisers, and note who you will need to contact.

2. Contact each portal and ask for information on monthly traffic statistics and a breakdown of people looking for opportunities on the site by industry and by investment range (and any other demographic information the site may have in terms of gender, age, or net worth, to compare to your ideal franchisee profile). Those that have the highest traffic of the types of candidates that match your ideal franchisee profile, your industry, and your investment range should be prioritized.

3. It is then time to negotiate (yes, all portals negotiate). Although I prefer shorter contract terms, I also concede that it takes a good three to four months before you can make a determination, because the real test of a good site is that one of the leads results in a sale or progresses far enough in the sales process to suggest that a future sale will result. Therefore, my preference is to agree to a three-month contract term whereby I get four months of leads for the price of three months if it is a fixed monthly rate.

4. I prefer sites that charge me per lead generated and that allow me to pay more to apply filters for higher-quality leads based on investment range and/or net worth criteria. Most, if not all, will also let you apply filters to exclude states in which you are not interested in franchising so that you get (and pay for) only those leads you can use.

5. Sites are beginning to pop up that let you receive an unlimited number of leads free of charge until one of the leads purchases a franchise, at which time you pay a success fee of $6,000 to $12,000. (This appears to be the way the portal market is heading—or at least it should be.) The fee varies according to when you join the portal and how difficult your concept is to find leads for (remember, there are fewer leads for higher investment levels, and fewer for non-home-based). This model

is a no-risk proposition, and the risk-reward proposition is akin to the broker model, in which you pay only for success. If these new portals invest in solid prequalifying, so the leads are of high quality, I think they could sign up the majority of franchisors.

I recommend trying anywhere between two and five portals for four months (paying for three) as an initial start. Once you select a few portals to try, be sure to put as much effort as is feasible into developing your website content. You will only have a few seconds to grab a prospect's attention, so hit the highlights and use bullet points!

Print

Some franchisors have good success with print advertising. For instance, I see newspaper advertisements for Volvo Rents and Aaron's all the time, so it must work for them. We have not been successful with print advertising, and it is expensive. We have only closed a handful of sales with prospects who found us through a print ad, and the costs for the completions were much higher than $9,000.

We had better success advertising in *Entrepreneur* magazine, once we had been ranked in the January edition that features the Franchise 500 (which took until we had five years of history). When we tried it before then, it didn't yield a sale for us. I think print ads probably deliver many indirect leads, just as PR does, because prospects see the advertisement and then visit the website.

Since print requires such a large investment, I recommend working with the company that designed your website to set up a unique landing page (a copy of your website but with a unique URL) and use this in the print ad so you can track the specific number of leads that found you through the print advertisement. I do not see print as a cost-effective option for most franchisors in the first few years of franchising, although *Entrepreneur's*

Franchise 500 issue can be viable once you are to a stage where you feel you will make the list.

Lesser-Known Lead Sources

Though they aren't as "sexy" as portals, franchisee satisfaction survey tools and their websites nevertheless do generate leads. I believe in using these tools first and foremost to assure us that we are focusing on the right activities and investments to always be improving franchisee satisfaction, our model, and our franchisees' results (this topic is covered in more detail in chapter 10). Also, being able to share how the franchisees rate the franchisor with a prospect is a powerful tool to improve completion ratios. In addition, both Franchise Business Review (FBR) and FranSurvey generate leads. We value both tools and feel that the strengths of each, though different, yield feedback that is worth its weight in gold. With a brilliant marketer at its helm, FBR generates more leads. FranSurvey "certifies" a much smaller number of franchisors because of the stringent criteria and the anonymity of the survey. (Its founder is a former franchisee who prioritizes the process and science above any marketing consideration.) We pay to use both services, alternating between them so that we are surveying every six months.

Brokers

I am a big fan of brokers (or "consultants," depending on their preferred vernacular). One of our first five franchisees came through a broker, and he is an absolutely wonderful, high-performing franchisee. It is unusual to have a broker network represent you before you have at least 10 open units, and even then you might go through a rigorous process to be accepted into what they call "inventory."

Now it's time for a story that shows how persistence can pay off when it comes to brokers. I began calling on all of the big broker networks, including the highly respected FranNet, in mid-2005. I kept on contacting them and sending information and got a few of them to consider signing a contract just in case (after convincing them that there was no downside to them because most likely they would not be sending me leads).

Then one day I got a call from a broker with FranNet about a prospect of his who was a former hospital administrator and was interested in becoming a franchisee with a medical concept. I could tell that the broker was calling reluctantly. Fortunately he had all of my contact information from my repeated calls, e-mails, and overnight mailings to him. The FranNet broker said there was nothing else in the FranNet inventory that offered *medical* home care, and even though he tried to warn his prospect that we were new and therefore a huge risk, the prospect wanted to talk to us anyway. This was a huge break for us. Not only was it an opening to do business with a broker group with an amazing reputation, it was also a great opportunity to attract a high-quality franchisee. (I will refer to him as "John" to protect his privacy.)

We began talking with John over the next couple of months, and he flew into Chicago for our Join-the-Team Day (it was "Discovery Day" at that time). We connected right away, sharing the same values and a passion for high-quality care. This was a big decision for John, though, as we were a new franchisor and unproven. John asked me if, as a last step, I would meet a friend of his who lived in Chicago. He wanted this person he respected to provide feedback on whether joining us was a good decision. Of course, I would do anything (as long as it complied with franchise sales laws and regulations) I could to help John make the decision to join us. Then John told me his friend happened to be the managing partner for one of the "big four" CPA firms. I was nervous. For a CPA who began in public accounting, a meeting with a managing partner was a big deal.

I arrived for our lunch meeting a bit early and was shown to "his table."

Yes, he had a table, and his picture hung on the wall above it. I suddenly felt nauseated, and I couldn't bring myself to eat much during lunch. Our conversation started off a bit dicey when I asked what he thought about John joining our franchise and he said, "Like I have told John, I think he is smart enough to start this without you." From that point on, there was only one way to go—up!

I began discussing our model and the money that we had invested in the branding, securing trademarks, our technology, etc., and I compared that to the franchise fee and future royalties from a risk-reward standpoint. He asked a lot of questions and I answered every one. At the end, I asked whether he would tell John he should join us or to do it without us. (I had never been in sales, but J.D. says, "Always ask for the sale," so I did.) He smiled and said he would tell John he should move forward with us and he would also like to set up another meeting for his brother to meet me because he would also advise his brother to consider becoming a franchisee. (His brother did join, and he is still a franchisee performing well.)

This was such a pivotal point for us. First, FranNet took us into inventory after we closed that first sale, and they continue to be a major contributor to our growth. Second, we got John as a franchisee. John has been a great franchisee and a great friend from the beginning. He's a top performer and, more important, he's invested in making the brand better. We began the chapter talking about selecting the right franchisees, but this story seems like the right place to thank FranNet for finding us one of our best. I was so proud and delighted to announce John's selection as Franchisee of the Year in 2010 that I cried a bit as I presented it—and got my hug.

We have also had great success with FranChoice, The Entrepreneur Source, and MatchPoint in terms of the number of franchisees that have joined us. As long as a broker network has a good reputation in terms of franchise compliance and understands that the franchise sales rules apply to them (including the rules regarding financial performance representations), then we are happy to work with multiple networks and the independent brokers too.

Generally the quality of our franchisees is higher through the brokers, which is why we are such huge advocates of using them. While we are increasing our online investment to bring our balance of new franchisees to more of a 50/50 (broker/non-broker) percent split, we expect to still see a large portion of our continued growth result from broker leads.

Once you have approximately 10 franchisees and you are interested in looking at the broker networks, you should begin contacting the networks to find out how to submit your information to be considered. Each will have its own process. Be persistent. As cautioned in the section related to outsourcing franchise sales, be careful about the terms you agree to. I have been unwilling—and always will be—to accept terms in which I have to pay a portion of my royalties for a period of time or in perpetuity.

Referrals

Certainly we were lucky to get a referral early on by having John's friend and advisor refer his brother to us. Recognizing that referrals are the lowest cost of acquiring a new franchisee, I set out to craft an internal referral program.

 BRIGHT IDEA:

I strongly recommend being more intentional about this activity by planning, disclosing, and communicating a referral program.

We added a referral program to our franchise disclosure document so that we are able to pay a modest amount to any individual who directly refers a prospect to us who winds up becoming a franchisee. You need to ensure that your process for selecting franchisees doesn't change and that the prospect is just as rigorously screened as any other prospect; an existing franchisee should never be able to influence the decision—and become a franchise *seller's agent*—as part of the referral program. You should also discuss this program with your attorney to ensure that the amount offered is not material in any manner that could cause a franchisee to do more than merely refer a candidate as part of the process.

Here are a couple of things you should do in addition to establishing your own referral program. First, make sure your franchisees know the rules regarding the referral program: To receive the financial reward, the referral must be direct to the franchisor and not to the broker who placed the referring franchisee. Otherwise, only the broker benefits and your referring franchisee will be disappointed when you explain that you can't pay her and why. Second, understand that franchisees do not refer prospects solely for the money, so be sure you recognize the referring franchisee publicly as frequently and in as big a way as possible (newsletters, system calls, and at conferences).

Closing Thoughts

We all want to grow our systems by adding franchisees, particularly as we start up our business. In closing this section, I want to revisit a word of advice and share one of my great ideas that I will use with future franchise brand launches.

First, I want to reiterate and lend my two cents to the advice you get from everyone to not sell to family or friends; it is absolutely true. And, no, I didn't listen to it either, but I wish I had. I also recommend against selling to parents wanting to buy their adult child a business or a sibling wanting to buy another sibling a business.

My great idea is to give away the first few franchises. You heard that right. Offer the first few for absolutely no initial franchise fee. You should run this idea by your franchise attorney, of course, to ensure that he advises you on how to do this legally and helps you understand the disclosure issues. BrightStar's intent with our next foray into creating new brands is to offer the first few free of charge to gain even greater collaboration with a new brand.

. . .

In the next section, we will focus on executing for sustainability. Several elements are necessary for the success of a franchise model. Franchisors need to understand how they really make their money. Franchisors also need to train franchisees well and have a relentless pursuit of continuously improving franchisee unit economics. The long-term ability to consistently improve requires all of the franchisees and employees working together to achieve a common goal. Consequently, I will continue to focus on building an intentional culture to enable this.

Moreover, many of the strategies, systems, and support services that we will discuss in the next section relate to a central theme—accelerating a franchisee's time to breakeven. We focus on improving franchisee unit economics, but the reality is that if we can't help a franchisee start fast and stay strong, she will run out of capital on the five-yard line. You will see that our emphasis on training, fast-start initiatives like BrightStart, early communication, and benchmarking are all centered around improving early outcomes. How a franchisee does early on is a strong predictor of likely success down the road. For those franchisees who do not get off to a strong start (which can occur when the franchisee selects the wrong initial role and then is unable or unwilling to perform the activities to be successful in that role) or when one gets a flat tire along the way, we will discuss specific strategies such as "boost" programs, financial exceptions, territory right-sizing, formal diagnostic reviews, and, when necessary, resale programs that we use to assist franchisees in correcting their course.

SECTION 4

EXECUTING FOR SUSTAINABILITY

CHAPTER 8

How Does the Franchisor Make Money?

Franchising is a business unto itself, and understanding the revenue model is important. It is critical to understand how you as the franchisor make money and how you accelerate financial gain over time by making the right investments, having the right conversations, and making the difficult but necessary decisions that move the business forward.

Soon after you begin attending franchise conferences, you'll most likely sit in on a session in which the speaker asks the group, "How does the franchisor make money?" Without fail, "franchise fees" is always the first answer given. Other common answers include "royalties," "goods," and "technology fees." But the reality of the franchise industry is that most franchisor profit is generated from royalties. Though most conferences focus on franchise sales, lead generation, and closing deals, I think more should be dedicated to maximizing both franchisee unit economics and franchisor royalties.

The most successful and sustainable franchisors recognize that royalties are—or should be—where they make the majority of their profit. We know that we actually *lose* money on the sale of a franchise: It takes about 22 months, on average, before we achieve breakeven on the addition of a single-unit franchisee. With this level of investment in the selection, training, opening, and support of franchisees, it is critical to select great ones. Royalty dollars are not created equal. Top performers pay the most and consume the least resources—and vice versa for underperformers. Pay close attention to the best practices shared in this book about building a successful franchise system and selecting the right franchisees; otherwise you could easily go upside down, building a system with unqualified franchisees that generate little in royalties and that cost too much to support to remain sustainable.

As a franchisor the most important achievement in your life cycle is the point at which you reach royalty self-sufficiency, the point at which all overhead costs are covered by royalties and there is no longer pressure to earn franchise fees. To calculate royalty self-sufficiency, subtract from royalty revenues all of your operating expenses for all functions except franchise sales. If the number is positive (i.e., revenues exceed expenses for operations other than franchise sales), then you have reached royalty self-sufficiency. If it is negative, then you must grow royalty revenues to reach this milestone. The magnitude of the negative number will give you an idea of how long that should take.

Generally, when a franchisor has 100 units open, he should be at or near the point of royalty self-sufficiency. I like to see franchisors get there in less than five years, with a goal of three years if all plans are executed well. A dear friend, Ron Feldman, CEO of Franchise America Finance, teases me that I probably knew the precise moment we would reach royalty self-sufficiency to the minute. Well, we planned to be there in November 2008, and we were essentially there within six weeks of plan—and that was during a recession!

Sometimes, however, you consciously make the decision to move away from this milestone if critical investments are needed. We were royalty self-sufficient (what a great place to be!) in the first half of 2009; then, knowing we had achieved it once, and with full knowledge and support of our bank, we increased costs to add a new program in July 2009 to help our franchisees ramp up faster and counteract the downturn in the economy. (I talk more about our BrightStart program in chapter 9.)

BRIGHT IDEA:

You should know both the point at which you'll attain royalty self-sufficiency and what is needed to get there. If new program costs delay that, you should know what incremental royalty the program must achieve to give you a positive ROI on the cost of the program and get you back to royalty self-sufficiency.

The key takeaway here is simple. Royalties are derived from the unit economics of franchisees, and chapters 9 through 11 are about what we do, from intake to ongoing support, to maximize franchisees' ability to build revenue. This chapter focuses on the ways in which a franchisor maximizes royalties. Why? Because investing in franchisee success and working together to maximize franchisee revenues and bottom-line profitability is the fastest way for a franchisor to be successful.

Sometimes it feels like the road less traveled when I compare my staff-to-franchisee ratios to other franchisors, but franchisee revenue maximization clearly leads to royalty maximization for the franchisor. Also, if franchisees are making a good return they will validate favorably to prospects, they will want to consider adding franchise units, and they may want to become a franchisee of other concepts that you might start. Focusing on the franchisee is the best way for a franchisor to make money, avoid litigation, and sleep well at night. This is the beauty of franchising— the more the franchisee wins, the more the franchisor wins too.

The biggest way to ensure maximized royalties is to remain committed to awarding a franchise only to those who are most likely to succeed. We talked in the last chapter about building your ideal franchisee profile and looking for and selecting franchisees who meet the criteria. In addition to selecting strong franchisees, here are proven strategies to maximize royalties (which I'll describe in detail in the next section):

1. Invest in a strong start for your franchisees.
2. Be proactive in communication; don't postpone the tough conversations with new franchisees.
3. Offer "boost" programs to support struggling franchisees, and then have a clear plan for what to do should the boost not work.
4. Be prepared to make acceptable exceptions for high-performance and high-attitude franchisees: They are your proven commodities.
5. Review the list of your franchisees regularly and identify the bottom performers and build plans to support them up or out.
6. Right-size the franchisee's operation and/or geography to match the skills and capitalization of the franchisee.

With some franchisees, you will need to implement more than one of these strategies simultaneously. With others, you may need one strategy now and another in 6 to 12 months. In my view, strategy 5 is the most important advice for new franchisors. If a franchisee is below goal, you must invest to support her efforts to move from average to top performer. We define the goal; franchisees and support personnel have access to real-time statistics to show the franchisee's weekly sales performance compared to goal for the week and for inception-to-date. The franchisees must do the work and make the commitment while we provide the resources to help their effort be effective. If a franchisee's performance is too poor and he is not putting in the effort, lacks accountability for the results, or doesn't have a positive attitude (the single largest common trait among top performers is optimism and/or positive attitude), move him out of the system (it is best if this can be done mutually, but unilaterally may be the only option under certain circumstances).

Strategies to Maximize Royalties

It took me a while to realize that I couldn't help everyone become successful and that not everyone will help themselves to become successful. Some franchisees believe they can handle a particular role but later realize that they can't. When this happens, they usually hire someone else to do it. Unfortunately, with an owner-operator business model, by design, if they hire to fill every role early on, the model doesn't work, either from execution or from proper capitalization. Owner-operator franchises like ours *initially* need the owner's time and passion to succeed. Many franchise systems, including ours, allow a franchisee to develop his team over time and to transition out of working *in* the business to fulfill a higher-level leadership role of working *on* the business.

The sooner you determine whether your franchisee is in it to win it— or not—the better for both of you, especially the franchisee. So let's look more closely at the strategies for supporting franchisees to enable them to reach their potential (and produce royalties), and when and how to suggest they follow a different path, if necessary.

Invest in a Strong Start

In chapter 9 you will see how we on-board new franchisees from the program perspective. Here I want to review the strong correlation between how a franchisee starts and her long-term potential. Unfortunately, franchisees who have a slow start often cannot recover from it. Our analysis reveals that, in general, franchisees who start strong stay strong. Because of strong franchisee performance in their second year and beyond, the critical breakthrough for us and our franchisees was in getting them started strong. In networking with other franchisors, this theory appears to hold up across brands and across industries.

Our senior leadership team has key scorecard items that we watch and strive to improve annually. Among them are three goals, with the ultimate goal of having happy, successful franchisees: Maximize franchisee unit economics, shorten the franchisee time to breakeven, and minimize the time period that a franchisee is open without billing. I challenged our team during the down economy of early 2009 to identify tools, resources, and/or programs that we could implement to impact these three goals. Two of my senior staff worked closely together and mapped out a plan for BrightStart.

The team came up with a launch program to help franchisees ramp up sales sooner through a combination of investments for (1) additional travel costs related to more on-site visits; (2) additional personnel to support preopening activities, such as territory management and reviewing the preselling process to diagnose the approach and results of sales calls; (3) personnel for the first three or four months to monitor sales activities and results and to ensure that key behaviors were formed; (4) technology to standardize the external sales process and to identify problems at any stage of the sales process; and (5) agreement by the franchisee to participate in and comply with the requirements of the program.

The travel, personnel, and technology were expenses, with an estimated 18 months to pay back the incremental costs, but we knew the program could have a significant impact for the franchisees who took advantage of the additional resources. Franchisees who do not follow the requirements of the BrightStart program are removed from the program until they have a dedicated salesperson who will follow the program. I approved the program, and we launched the first trial in July 2009. Based on the feedback we gathered from franchisees, we continued to refine the program.

The program improved franchisee results so much that payback on the incremental recurring costs (travel and personnel) occurred in less than eight months.

BRIGHT IDEA:
Tracking the realization of benefits from any new programs is critical.

Monitoring program results will encourage you to form the complementary habits of empowering employees to identify ways to help franchisees and holding the employee responsible for the results, to offset the incremental costs within a reasonable period of time. Remember, you must be financially healthy for the brand to survive and thrive. We benchmark how much we are already investing in support, so increases to that amount must demonstrate ROI by increasing franchisees' revenues enough that the increases in royalties cover the additional support costs.

Because the BrightStart program had strong measurable goals and the team responsible was held accountable, we viewed the money we spent on travel, personnel, and technology as an investment rather than an expense. It changed our franchisees' track records (for those who complied with the program requirements) and therefore improved our own royalty opportunity. In today's age of more limited resources, we must be prudent in investing in these types of programs; we can no longer merely look at increasing expenses by a certain percentage per year in line with revenue growth. Ultimate success for our franchisees and for us as the franchisor requires an investment in the things that drive improved franchisee performance.

I want to return to an aspect of our program that may have been too subtle in the previous discussion. The BrightStart program works well and has been able to deliver an ROI because *franchisee accountability* has been built into the program. To receive these additional resources free of charge, franchisees are required to make sales calls. We remove franchisees from the program if they are not doing their part. This ensures that we are investing in those who will use the resources to drive their revenue—and ours. We will allow a franchisee who was removed to restart BrightStart once he fixes whatever had prevented him from following the program requirements.

Sometimes we've been guilty of spending too many resources on those who won't do their part and then not having the right amount of resources for the franchisees who are following the model. With the BrightStart program, we got it right by being clear about what we would do for our franchisees and what we expected from them in return.

We continue to look for ways to improve the BrightStart program and look for new programs or resources to help franchisees start stronger. In a tight capital market, the longer it takes for a franchisee to reach breakeven, the harder it will be for her to manage her cash and the more difficult it will be for her to access capital until she can show positive cash flow.

As you contemplate developing your own program for a stronger start, evaluate the key aspects of the business model that have the biggest impact on franchisee profitability. For us, sales call volume and following the sales methodology (including asking for the sale rather than just dropping off brochures) was the single greatest key performance indicator for franchisee success. Knowing how important sales calls are, we created a two-pronged program to improve sales results. We built accountability into the issue of the quantity and effectiveness of sales calls, and we built a support system for salespeople. We undertook a program to coach the salesperson regarding who to call on and how to advance the call to a buying decision, and to role-play to increase the salesperson's confidence. Your franchise system may have other key performance indicators—the important point is that they should determine how you allocate extra resources to help your franchisees get off to a strong start.

Communicate Proactively

All franchisees should want to be successful—that is, operate a profitable and sustainable business. Unfortunately, as with buying stocks, there are no guarantees in starting or buying a business. While I believe (and franchise industry research generally supports this position) that opening a franchise business is more likely to succeed than starting as an independent from scratch, not every franchisee will be able to do it.

I have had to accept, too, that a small percentage of franchisees welcome the mutual realization that the business isn't right for them or that it isn't the right time in their life for the business. They seem relieved when I initiate "the conversation." There is also a statistical likelihood that franchisees will have health issues, get divorced, or encounter some other upset. When men and women meet with significant life changes, they often find it difficult to focus on the business and to determine what needs to be done.

AVOID THIS PITFALL:

As I matured as a franchisor, I realized that every day I delayed "the conversation" cost the franchisee—who I was actually trying to protect—frustration and money.

As we built our field support organization, I hired staff who said they were willing and able to have tough conversations with franchisees and hold them accountable. Giving tough love is the right medicine to get the business back on track or to help the franchisee exit quickly and/or recover as much money as possible by selling his business. As you build your field support organization and reassess it over time, the ability to have tough conversations, document solid action plans, and obtain franchisee buy-in (and a signature on the required action plan) are skills that must be demonstrated—a lack of these skills and actions is a clear indication that you need to make a change in the team. Train early and often to this expectation and inspect what you expect—your success and that of your franchisees is strengthened by it.

The sooner you can have an honest conversation with the franchisee and identify why a business is struggling, the sooner a plan can be built. Asking the right questions will help you determine whether or not the struggle is temporary. If it is, you can help the franchisee with additional resources, motivation, mentoring, or possibly a temporary realignment of financial obligations. For instance, the franchisee might simply need to hire someone to fill a skill set that he is missing. On the other hand, if the struggle is related to a lack of skills, a lack of capital, or an improper fit, then it is a permanent struggle, and the franchisee would probably prefer to exit the system—or he *should* exit the system. The longer an unsuccessful franchisee bleeds cash, the more the likelihood of selling the business, or selling it at a good price, declines because potential buyers will wonder if the problem is indeed the operator and not the model or the market. The sooner the plan to exit is laid out and executed, if that is the right course of action, the better for everyone.

Offer "Boost" Programs

As I've shown, our attitude is that if the franchisee is committed to putting in the time and doing the work with a positive attitude, we will provide additional resources to help her improve her business. This approach is true for new franchisees as well as for existing franchisees.

We didn't implement BrightStart until mid-2009, but by then we already had some franchisees who had struggled in the beginning, or who had been successful but had stumbled a bit because of employee turnover or a health issue. In late 2009 we began to identify ways in which some franchisees could benefit from a modified BrightStart program to give them a "boost." We identified owners who had been open longer than nine months but were not performing to the level of our expectations or theirs.

We offered them the boost program gratis, as long as they agreed to do the work and meet the requirements. This ensured that both parties were committed to an investment of time to help the business improve its results. Most franchisees took us up on the offer and benefited from the resources.

About a year later, we reviewed franchisees again and identified a new set of 10 to whom we offered the program. Evaluating the performance of franchisees is part of our DNA, and we are committed to offering additional resources to improve results. We have built in the necessary criteria to ensure that we don't wind up with the franchisee trying to transfer the responsibility for his results to us. As long as the franchisee owns the action plan and follows it, we will guide him in what work he needs to do and how to do it.

As you contemplate initiating your own boost program, evaluate the key aspects of the business model that may be missing in the particular franchisee's execution of the model, thus causing him to underperform. You can identify an entire group in need of a boost program by evaluating the time frame in which you expect your franchisees to reach breakeven if they follow the model. At this stage (measured in months), evaluate the revenue levels of the group of franchisees open; those below 75 percent of the expected level should be considered for incremental resources. Use the same focus to accelerate your franchisees' results as you developed in your strong-start program. Include rules of accountability in your boost program, and if the franchisee is unable to do his part and follow your accountability guidelines, proceed to proactive communication of his need to exit the system.

Make Exceptions for High Performers

Sometimes you need to consider taking more extreme measures than offering a boost program, especially if a franchisee runs into cash-flow issues due to a decrease in business. Although we don't have unlimited cash reserves and do have a brand to sustain and protect, on rare occasions we have offered a helping hand when a franchisee would have failed by temporarily restructuring monies they owed us or by loaning them money until other funds were secured or until their business was sold.

Attorneys will caution against helping out franchisees financially, and we have to be very careful about establishing a precedent in the way we treat similarly situated franchisees. While I am careful to not risk legal liability by trying to go above and beyond to help a franchisee, I will bet on the winning horse that has a proven jockey. During economic downturns, franchisors will be tested more frequently as to how far they will go to help a struggling franchisee who had once been a high performer with a great attitude and had maintained accountability for the results, both good and not so good. For example, one of our "Top 10" performers—who served on our franchise advisory council and consistently gives back to other franchisees by mentoring and sharing best practices—suffered a health issue. At about the same time, he had some turnover in his team. The business slid because he was unable to make sales calls for several months until his health improved, and he struggled to make payroll because sales had declined. Because he is a known performer, a great person, and a great franchisee with a positive attitude and strong accountability, BrightStar (which is me, essentially, since I own 100 percent of the business) loaned him money until his SBA loan was funded. In less than three months, he was back in the "Top 10," got his loan funded, and repaid all that we had loaned him. The franchisee–franchisor relationship transcends the terms of the agreement.

My philosophy for BrightStar's franchisee family is simply this: We help one another and go the extra mile in an extreme time of need when we know that the results will be different—better—within a short period of time. Top performers are a proven commodity; they have the skills and attitude to be successful again if someone merely invests and believes in them. As long as the franchisee conducts himself as a good steward of the brand and maintains accountability for the business results (rather than blaming others), we will do our best to help identify a win-win solution.

Review the Bottom Performers

Bottom performers come in different packages. Most franchisors address the franchisees who are not following the model, are noncompliant, and therefore have low revenues. I say this carefully, because some franchisors attribute all franchisee failures to the franchisees' not following the model rather than looking at themselves. The first place to look when evaluating a franchisee's under-performance is what, if anything, in the system contributed to the breakdown, such as recruiting, training, operations support, and so on. With this evaluation and a commitment to assist in any and all areas to bridge this deficiency, it is also appropriate to evaluate what deficiencies of the franchisee, in the commitment level, attitude, leadership capabilities, etc., could be contributing to her failure.

We identify bottom performers based on either not meeting revenue goals or having a bad attitude. Poor attitudes and/or hostile communications toward corporate staff, vendors, etc., are like a bad flu infecting everyone around. There is no easy way to get strong revenue producers with poor attitudes to leave the system if they are compliant. Sometimes offering an incentive to sell can be a great investment to get someone like this out of the system. Or sometimes peer pressure by other franchisees will improve the poor attitude or help the franchisee self-select out.

As stated in section 3, I caution against awarding a franchise to prospects with overly large egos or with unrealistic expectations. In both situations the individual often demonstrates a poor attitude. Sometimes you find out too late. I once had a franchisee who had been forced out of a company where he was making $300,000 a year. After three years as a franchisee, he measured the return on the franchise against the $900,000 he would have earned in his former career. Despite setting no expectations for this candidate as to earnings and not providing any information other than what was in the FDD, his concept of the opportunity cost turned a good performer into a difficult franchisee who would never be happy with us. So what happens when someone like this gets into your system? Every situation is unique. All I know is that I finally freed myself from trying to live up to *his* unrealistic expectations so that I could use that energy to focus on the franchisees who appreciated the help and growth that our support could provide.

Remember, a customer's or an employee's bad experience with a poor performer damages the brand's reputation, and that is unfair to you and the other franchisees who are following the model. Protecting the brand is the key responsibility of the franchisor, and getting noncompliant franchisees out of the system must be a key priority. The noncompliant franchisee needs to be put on notice or, depending on the circumstances, terminated in accordance with the appropriate legal requirements.

Right-Size the Franchisee's Operation

If you choose to offer single-unit as well as multi-unit franchise opportunities, I recommend building a separate process for reviewing the performance of each type. For example, not every franchisee will have the leadership abilities or capitalization necessary to run multiple locations. The model often changes when the franchisee scales up to multiple locations; multi-unit ownership is not merely *more of running one* but, rather, is an entirely different model that requires separate training and infrastructure, as well as new franchisee skills, roles, responsibilities, etc.

Multi-unit operators need to be adept at developing their teams to handle key responsibilities. When a franchisee progresses to multiple locations, he will be spread too thin to be the sole individual contributor that he was as a single-unit operator. Multi-unit operators must likewise have the proper capitalization to invest in building the right team in location two and three; simply having the geography without the team to maximize its potential is not enough.

BrightStar had to build a review process to assist franchisees in evaluating what would be needed to keep the larger territory and maximize its potential if they had or could acquire the requisite skills and had the proper capitalization for multi-unit operations, as well as to create options for what to do if they could not acquire the skills and were not properly capitalized to expand. For franchisees who lacked the capital to fully staff the additional locations, we created a win-win opportunity for them to sell off the additional locations to new franchisees through the resale process. Allowing franchisees to sell their additional locations and still remain in our system as a single-unit operator created a solid financial opportunity: Franchise fees have increased each year, and additional territories cost less than first locations. When selling at current prices, the franchisee recovers cash and generally makes a return on the amount that had been invested in additional territories when fees were lower.

I like multi-unit ownership because of the scalability it offers. Multi-unit ownership allows the franchisee to leverage resources across multiple locations. For the franchisor, multi-unit franchising allows field staff to make only one visit to a franchisee who represents the revenue potential of multiple locations. While there is a tremendous opportunity for the franchisee and the franchisor, the effect can be the opposite if the franchisee isn't focused on developing her team to assume responsibility for the results of the first location, and then a second team to assume responsibility for the results of the second location, and so on.

I also see the expansion into new franchise brands as another way to achieve scalability. My highest-performing employees will have greater opportunity for development and promotion because they will be able to move up in a different brand. Multi-concept ownership can create opportunity for the franchisee to expand and diversify into additional brands and simultaneously create an opportunity for the franchisee to attract and retain employees who see the opportunity to grow with a larger operation. This means, though, that the franchisee must allocate time to develop and empower the team to take on increasing levels of responsibility so that the franchisee has the bandwidth to take on more locations and/or more brands. Buying additional territories (or units) or into additional brands without having the right team to leverage the opportunity is a waste of energy, money, and talent.

In summary, looking at a franchisee's capitalization and skills holistically, as well as trying to identify ways to create win-win solutions, can uncover the need for action plans for the franchisee to train and develop staff to maximize territory potential or to right-size a territory downward while creating an infusion of cash from the sale of the additional territories.

· · ·

We have looked at multiple strategies to maximize royalties, so now let's spend a little time looking at some of the key franchisor metrics and the plans necessary to constantly improve them. For franchisors the biggest opportunity is finding the right balance between providing support to drive franchisee results and controlling infrastructure costs.

BRIGHT IDEA:

Understanding where resources will be best deployed for the highest ROI is key to maximizing franchisor profitability.

Franchisor Key Metrics

Experience shows that there are key metrics to watch to improve the sustainability and growth of the franchisor. These metrics comprise a cross section of revenue, profitability, and efficiency measures that enable you to assess performance over time and to prioritize what to focus on to achieve top quartile performance in your industry. I use a review of my competitors' metrics (as well as a review of top performing franchisors across the service sector obtained from FRANdata), by obtaining their FDDs and building a model to calculate their revenues per dollar of payroll, EBITDA as a percentage of revenue, and so forth, to set annual budgeting goals and multiyear improvement goals for my team, and then empower my team to propose what levers to pull to reach the desired outcomes.

As discussed earlier in this chapter, the point of royalty self-sufficiency is the magical time in the life cycle of a franchisor. If you have already launched your franchise operation, be sure to ask your accountant to add a row labeled "royalty self-sufficiency" on your financial statements for the calculation of royalties less the expenses not associated with franchise sales. When the number is positive, you are no longer dependent on new franchise sales to be profitable. Until the number is positive, the business is on shaky ground, because you must sell franchises or have access to additional capital to keep the lights on.

The next metric to watch is the contribution margin per franchisee. This is measurable by taking royalty revenues less the department costs related to supporting all franchisees (not the departments focused solely on new franchisees) and dividing this number by the average number of franchisees open during the year. We are looking for an improvement in this number to measure our scalability over time by ensuring that the gap between revenue and expenses continues to widen by generating more revenues than we add expenses over time. This is a high-level measurement of the success of new programs in which we ramp up royalties and the competency and effectiveness of field support personnel.

Once a year I also like to review the cost to open a single-unit franchise and the number of months on average for BrightStar to reach breakeven with a new franchisee. To calculate my cost to open a single franchise, I look at the total amount of initial franchise fees in the year divided by the number of franchises sold in that year and subtract from it (1) the cost of goods sold (advertising and broker fees) divided by the number of franchises sold in that year; (2) the full costs of cost centers that are primarily responsible for on-boarding new franchises—such as franchise sales, learning and development or training, BrightStart, and preopening—divided by the number of franchises sold in that year; and (3) the other departments such as support center, field support, etc., divided by the number of average franchises open in that year (this adjusts the number to be smaller because those resources are supporting all franchisees and not just the new ones).

This review can be applied to see how many months of royalties on average it takes to offset the cost to open a single-unit franchise. Some franchisors whose opening support is more modest or who did not use brokers to find franchisees can reach breakeven very soon or can actually make money on the sale of a franchise. For BrightStar, our time to breakeven has ranged from 16 months to 22 months based on our franchisees' results and on the cost of new programs such as BrightStart and our large infrastructure of one employee for every three franchisees.

The next metric on the monthly financial statements that I review shows the revenue per dollar of payroll; this is a calculation of all revenues divided by all payroll costs. The goal is to increase this number over time. This number reflects the scalability of the organization based upon the ability of an investment in employees (payroll dollars) to drive an even larger increase in the amount of revenues. This is a key metric that I also use to compare our organization to peers in the same industry, regardless of their size, to hold our team accountable for being the most efficient in the use of our resources. This metric is great for franchisors, regardless of the size of the organization, because it normalizes for size to really just focus on the efficiency of resource utilization.

The last two metrics relate to ratios of earnings before interest, taxes, depreciation, and amortization (EBITDA) as a function of total revenues and as a function of royalty revenues alone. The first metric will show what percentage of revenue falls out to the bottom line. In networking conversations with other financial-oriented franchisors and/or private equity groups that own franchise companies, EBITDA as a percentage of total revenues upward of 30 percent is ideal and a best practice is 60 percent. This is the metric that I use as the goal for the next year's budgets, working the organization year-by-year incrementally toward 60 percent. We moved past 30 percent in 2010 and will move past 40 percent in 2011, nearing 50 percent in the last few months of the year. This should allow us to achieve at least 50 percent, with an opportunity to approach 60 percent, in 2012.

For organizations that are deriving a significant amount of net revenue from the sale of new franchises, the profitability can be masked by net "new-deal" revenue (measured by franchise fees less advertising costs, broker fees, and commissions). This is why I began looking at EBITDA as a percentage of royalty revenues alone to ensure that we are improving this area as well and setting an even higher bar than for EBITDA as a percentage of total revenues. While we have fairly consistent net new-deal revenue achieved or budgeted in 2009–2011 (and therefore the EBITDA as a percentage of total revenues would not be misleading), I have ensured that both of these EBITDA metrics are on the monthly financials and that we budget these metrics and also review how we are performing compared to our budget goals and compared to our peers.

You'll remember from chapter 4 the importance of building a high-performance culture for growth, and that is the key to achieving financial results, too. We align our budgeting process to drive the improvement in the key metrics of the franchisor by providing an opportunity for stretch goals for the employees to increase their quarterly bonus payout. When the company earns greater profits, then the employees' bonus opportunity increases. Let's look at our budgeting process a bit more and see if there are some takeaways for you to help drive an increase in your results—regardless of your industry and regardless of whether you are a franchisee, franchisor, or business considering franchising as an expansion option.

Budgeting Process: Good, Better, Best

Budgeting can be a great way to drive results. A lot of organizations see budgeting as a necessary annual task, but they fail to see a great opportunity to drive results through a thorough budgeting process. By aligning the goals of the organization and communicating to all employees what is needed to achieve them, an organization has the potential to achieve more.

We prepare three budgets, the primary difference among them being gross margin. I have used this process for years and have found it useful in my company-owned locations (before franchising), in the training of franchisees to set goals and prepare budgets, and in evolving the franchisor organization with the employees aligned to achieve more. In the years of the company-owned model and in the training of franchisees, I used three versions of the budget: worst case, target case, and best case. I used these three labels because we were at a stage in which the worst-case scenario had tight cash flows. As I launched the franchise and progressed beyond royalty self-sufficiency, I changed the labels to good-, better-, and best-case budgets.

When budgeting in a year in which cash flows could be tight under poor conditions, I take the worst-case, target-case, and best-case approach. The worst-case budget assumes the low end of probable sales so that I know our cash flow position. I provide the bank with this conservative scenario, what I call the "keeping the lights on" budget.

The target budget includes realistic revenue goals that require some stretch but are very achievable with an identified set of underlying key performance indicators, such as sales call activity, net promoter score or customer satisfaction, recruiting activity, etc.

The best-case budget includes the optimal sales goals I want my sales team focused on. I know that setting strong goals for sales and gaining 80–90 percent achievement will assure hitting my target "mid-point" budget. We still use a three-budget approach, but now that we are cash flow positive we have evolved from worst-case/target-case/best-case budgeting to good-/better-/best-case budgeting.

Since we may look at an initial public offering at some point in the future, we want our budget process to accomplish two key things: (1) Align focus on quarterly goals, since that is what analysts will be looking for if we are publicly traded, and (2) align the employees' earnings ability with driving additional profitability for the enterprise. The increase in bonus opportunity for the employees when moving from good budget to better budget to best budget is fully funded (plus a return for the enterprise) due to the increased profitability of the enterprise. The primary differences among the three budget scenarios are the number of new deals sold (and the associated advertising and broker fees) and royalties.

In the calculation of "good" revenue goals, the number of new deals is an industry average of deals per salesperson; the royalties are on the regression line, with the improvements in the current year over prior year calculated based upon the number of projected units generating revenues at historical performance levels, according to the number of months they will be open during the year. Thus, the good revenue goals are very realistic because we know that the goals are achievable if we keep doing what we are doing.

The "better" budget assumes increased efficiency per franchise salesperson in the number of new deals per person, and the royalty regression is increased by specific new revenue programs that will be the focus for the year. These increased efficiency goals for the franchise sales team will naturally populate the individual sales team members' individual goals and department goals. The specific new revenue programs developed to raise the regression potential for royalties will be aligned within the employee goals that are driving the programs or their implementation.

The "best" budget assumes a higher level of increased efficiency per franchise salesperson in the number of new deals per person; it also assumes that royalties are maximized for new programs and that franchisee revenues increase above historical levels for each franchisee.

The pool of overall money increases as the EBITDA budget goals progress from good to better to best. The dollars available are double at best compared to good, and they are 50 percent higher at better than good. Our employees then work together with their manager to set two individual goals for the quarter and two shared department goals (among multiple employees within or across departments), with each of the four goals representing one-fourth of the bonus opportunity. The goals are reviewed to ensure that they increase revenues or reduce costs to drive the overall budget goals. It is great to see the collective pride when together the whole team reaches the best results, as we did in the third quarter of 2010 and first quarter of 2011.

Aligning employees' abilities to influence the results of the organization with their own earning ability—in the short term and long term, as we discussed in chapter 4—is the key to building a sustainable organization. This is true in any industry, franchised or not. Ultimately, we have found this approach to be the key to maximizing how a franchisor makes money. We have also tried to align the goals of our corporate staff around initiatives that also improve franchisee unit economics. We want to link together the win-win for (1) the franchisees, in increased speed to breakeven and improved unit economics; (2) the franchisor, in increased royalties and earnings; and (3) the corporate staff in increased compensation, opportunities for growth, and bonus programs.

Closing Thoughts

You know from running your own business that time is precious and that optimal results are only achieved by understanding which key drivers in your business have the largest influence on financial success. We reviewed in this chapter how the franchisor makes money, underscoring that the success of the franchisees and that of the franchisor are interdependent. Therefore, it makes sense that the best way to improve the results of the franchisor is to focus on investing in the strong start of franchisees, communicating proactively and honestly, offering boost programs when needed, reviewing top performers and bottom performers, and taking the actions needed to increase the percentage of franchisees in the system that are giving their all to perform.

Furthermore, we discussed the actions needed to drive performance as well as the key metrics to watch to ensure that the actions have a measurable result on scalability and profitability. With the focus on maximizing the results of the franchisor, this chapter reviewed our budgeting process and how to align employee goals and compensation to stretch what is possible so the organization continues to achieve measurable progress.

· · ·

You now understand how important it is, given the interdependency of the franchisee's and the franchisor's successful results, that the franchisee start strong. We will discuss in the next chapter how to on-board your franchisees to accomplish this.

CHAPTER 9

On-boarding and Training

Your Franchisees

It is normal for the founder or leader of the company-owned locations to prepare the training curriculum and then train the franchisees, but this may not be your best option.

AVOID THIS PITFALL:

In retrospect, I was not the best person to develop the content and train my franchisees because I knew it so well that it was second nature to me.

I probably took it for granted that my franchisees understood the necessary terminology, the responsibilities, and the very basic processes of how the business worked. To the founder, everything is second nature: Compare this to golf. Often the founder is like the professional golfer who plays on the tour, a great performer. But professional golfers may not be great teachers, and that is why we have golf professionals who are not tour players but are better teachers of the game.

In chapter 5, you read about the importance of hiring an external company to assist you in developing your operations manuals and training procedures. We learned that while we could outline what to do and why it was important, only an outside consultant could identify what we were leaving out and ask the right questions. Moreover, an outside resource, a consultant, is much better initially from a cash-flow standpoint, because you can bring him in only when you need him. Once you begin selling franchises every month and are training monthly, you can consider hiring an internal resource for the training who can wear other hats when training is not going on. In addition to assisting with training, the outside resource could shadow your new internal resource until she is ready to lead training on her own.

Now we will walk through some of the major decisions that you will need to make to build a strong, sustainable foundation for on-boarding and supporting franchisees. I will try to shed some light on the competing factors when choosing the best tool versus a tool that may merely suffice until you see the system grow.

Support from Signing the Franchise Agreement to Opening

Every moment a franchisee spends prior to opening his business, he is burning through cash without an ability to earn revenue. In turn, you as the franchisor cannot earn royalties. Let's look at the steps you can take to get franchisees open as fast as possible and in a way that prepares them to hit the ground running.

Quick Introduction and Point Person

As soon as a franchisee signs the franchise agreement and parts with a large sum of money, it will be natural for anxiety and buyer's remorse to set in. The faster and more thorough you can be in welcoming the franchisee into the family and seeing to it that she has a point person—we call this position a preopening concierge—to reach in case she needs anything, the quicker her anxiety will turn into positive energy and a desire to work together for a successful start. When you first start out, you may not have one person who handles these franchisee relations, but the sooner you can afford to hire a person dedicated to this purpose, the better for you and your franchisees.

As you read in chapter 4, we added a preopening concierge in the beginning of 2007, when we had about 15 franchisees. Before then I was the primary point person.

AVOID THIS PITFALL:
Franchisees become accustomed to having the founder or CEO as the main point of contact, so breaking this connection may be difficult for them.

It's better not to establish that connection in the first place. Though the direct CEO-to-franchisee arrangement may be necessary in the beginning to conserve capital, the sooner you can shift the point person role from the CEO to someone else in the organization, the better, and the smaller the number of franchisees who also have to adjust.

The head of field support needs to have visibility to the performance of franchisees during the preopening phase. The regional field support person should be introduced early and have monthly meetings with the preopening concierge and franchisee to validate progression to an on-time and successful launch. If there are concerns over the franchisee's sense of urgency and/or abilities, the earlier this is identified and proactively and directly communicated by the regional field support director to the franchisee, the higher the likelihood to get the franchisee on-track before the "issues" cause a slow start. All identified issues should be documented in writing and an action plan developed that is acknowledged and committed to by the franchisee.

Training Programs

The moment you decide to franchise and become a franchisor, you are in the business of recruiting, training, consulting, and coaching to produce high-performing franchisees.

AVOID THIS PITFALL:

We learned early on that training programs should be administered by people who know how to develop business curriculum and understand adult learning principles.

That was not us; we were busy learning and doing other things. If you don't have that particular range of training expertise, you would be well advised to do what we did and hire someone who does. Similarly, if you do not understand business consulting techniques, get trained. And if you do not understand performance coaching to continually add value to high performers, I repeat—get trained.

When we first started, our training program took one week and included both the materials franchisees needed to get ready to open and the information they would need to run the business. We had been following this process for about 18 months when a franchisee suggested over lunch that we divide the program into two parts. The franchisee suggested that there be just a couple of days within 30 days of the franchisee joining the system to cover what a franchisee needs to know to understand the business, hire key employees, and get the business ready to open. Then, after a new franchisee had his team in place and the business was ready to open (probably 60 to 90 days after the first training), the team would come back for training in running the business. This matched what the franchisees needed to know with when they needed to know it, and they weren't overwhelmed with too much information at once. The change to two training sessions was a large improvement and probably cut down on a lot of frustration among franchisees and support personnel.

BRIGHT IDEA:

Our next largest breakthrough was the implementation of a learning management system (LMS) that allowed us to deliver training materials before the franchisees and their teams were in the classroom.

This pretraining was very effective in getting the franchisees to a certain level of knowledge, so that they all had similar quantities of information and could learn at the same pace. Similarly, this allowed each franchisee's team to learn the business, key terminology, customer types, etc., online and at their own pace before coming into the classroom. Once a student falls behind, it is nearly impossible to catch her up, and if you do try you hold everyone else back, it frustrates them, and ultimately you fail to cover all of the material thoroughly. We have continued to add to the curriculum and now have almost 100 hours of content.

I have discovered that many franchise systems do not train the franchisee's core team, even though they know how critical the team is to the franchisee's success. We always train the core team. We thought it was an unreasonable expectation that a new franchisee would learn all of this information about a new industry and be able to teach this content effectively to a new team. The new franchisee will not be an expert in the industry and how to run the business for quite some time, and it is unfair to put him in the position of having to train a team on information that he is not yet comfortable with.

The number of days and the number of times per year that we offer training has changed over time. Our classroom training includes three days of new-owner training and an additional five days of opening training for the franchisee and core team. This is approximately 64 to 72 hours of class-room training that we supplement with about 100 hours delivered through our LMS.

It took me a while to realize that I could significantly control costs and efficiency by not offering training every month.

I found that franchisees fared better when they started as part of a group, in which they could share their best practices and keep pace with one anoth-er's progress. As for Item 11 on the FDD regarding your training agenda (see chapter 2), you are allowed some flexibility regarding the number of hours for each component of training and the number of times per year that the training is offered. For instance, you are free to offer each training module a certain number of times per year or when a certain minimum number of franchisees can attend as long as you disclose that in Item 11.

Franchisee Support Team after Opening

Once the franchisee is ready to open, there is a subject matter expert (SME) transition from the preopening concierge to the BrightStart sales coach as activities transition from focusing on opening the business to growing the business. While the SME that is assigned to a franchisee may vary over time based upon the stage of the franchisee or a particular need, the primary relationship and oversight should be with the regional field support director (we didn't have this consistency in the beginning when we created the preopening role or the BrightStart team and the lack of holistic knowledge and accountability to a franchisee through field support was a glaringly missing component).

In the beginning, you and your team will wear multiple hats. One critical point to remember, however, is that your first 5 to 10 franchisees *have* to be successful. You need to be prepared for the 24/7 commitment that it takes to support them adequately. Ensure that you build in regular check-in visits to ensure that the franchisee has what he needs and is progressing according to plan. If he is not doing well, an early warning signal lets you step in with extra resources in time to get him over the hump.

Our support personnel model has changed dramatically over time, and we feel that we have finally optimized the model in terms of who we hire for each of our support teams. In fact, I think that understanding how to hire and use support teams is the aspect of franchising in which we have learned the most and evolved the most, and continue to do so.

Like many franchisors, BrightStar initially looked for field support personnel who walked on water. We needed them to be great at both sales and operations, in addition to having strong financial acumen and leadership ability. We would still be looking for these superhuman individuals today, or settling for a realistic subset of skills, if we hadn't transitioned to building multiple teams that had different backgrounds and skills and provided different services to the franchisees. It took us time to get it right—leveraging SMEs to assist field support by stepping in and providing a particular service for a specified period of time or for a specific skill set or function. The process is one of evolution.

Let's explore the three teams that we evolved and how they work together to provide the support franchisees need, when they need it. In the beginning, you won't have three support teams; as franchisor, you will build the separate roles over time. In the beginning, you can clearly define what two roles each person is handling and what the person's primary role will be (so you can hire to it) as you grow. Our three support teams are BrightStart, the support center, and field support.

GROW SMART, RISK LESS

BrightStart

I described the purpose of the BrightStart program in the prior chapter: to assist franchisees with ramping up through a dedicated team that has a strong focus on sales results. The BrightStart team, under the direction of field support, handles the ramp-up of a new franchisee for the first 17 weeks of operation, and it supports through a boost program those franchisees who are underperforming in light of their revenue goals after approximately nine months in operation. We seek personnel with a track record of sales success for the BrightStart team. This is critical because those support personnel who may be great at operations and finance will likely not be strong in sales, and vice versa.

Once we identified that we needed BrightStart focused on sales and field support focused on operations and leadership, we were able to develop job descriptions that actually represented real people rather than a make-believe superhuman who could conquer all areas.

BrightStart is designed to assist owners with building sales by providing weekly touch points for their first 17 weeks after opening, and to support owners in either an operations role or a sales role. We added new resources, including a salesperson on-boarding guide, to coach a salesperson hired by the franchisee, so franchisees could choose an operations role.

BrightStart is a comprehensive training and coaching program that combines a preopening focus on developing a franchisee's operating system, market and industry knowledge, and selling skills with a postopening support team to build sales competencies and provide back-office operations support. Preopening activities include classroom training, webinars, sales system technology, market knowledge, preselling the market, sales strategy, marketing planning, simulations, and role-playing. Postopening, activities include one-on-one phone coaching, in-person market visits (minimum of two), back-office operations support provided by the support center, and weekly performance reports highlighting progress to goals related to sales activity, referrals, new clients, and revenue.

The heart of the BrightStart program is the BrightResults sales process, which combines BrightStar's proprietary customer relationship management (CRM) technology with reporting, selling strategy, and mastery training. In addition to a full team of subject matter experts and trainers during the preopening process, the BrightStart sales specialist works with a new franchisee to guide her through the specific tasks and learning related to the sales process. These activities include training and implementation of BrightStar's CRM technology, preselling the market, identifying top sales prospects, zoning the territory for efficiency, ensuring training requirements are met, recruiting and on-boarding a sales manager, and progress reporting.

This incremental level of support also allowed us to expand the universe of prospects that could fit our model as franchisees. Prior to BrightStart we were only looking for franchisees who could sell. With the investment in this new program to assist franchisees in ramping up, we could expand to screening prospects with either operations or sales experience. It allowed us to focus first on the leadership abilities of a prospect. One of the side benefits of the BrightStart program is that having a franchisee start in the operations role makes him more effective as a multi-unit owner because he never needs to replace himself as the primary salesperson and avoids salesperson turnover in his market.

In addition to the implementation of BrightStart in 2009, we identified that our field support and BrightStart teams were getting a large number of back-office questions. We recognized that we could hire individuals with less but still relevant experience (at a lower salary) to handle these administrative questions and evaluated the launch of a new support center team in 2010, which we will discuss further in the next section.

Support Center

The launch of the support center had multiple benefits, many of which we didn't foresee at the outset. We improved franchisee satisfaction because franchisees no longer had to figure out who to call for assistance because every administrative and technology question and/or need was directed to the support center. We could also identify opportunities for improvements in training, technology, or communications on the basis of the frequency of questions. By incorporating a system for franchisees to request support online, we improved our efficiency for handling requests, with improved visibility and accountability for timely responses, as well as for tracking them.

The support center handles all technology questions related to our proprietary system and ancillary systems such as the financial software. The support center also handles all questions related to finding marketing tools, vendor contacts, and rate or contract information online. If a particular office asks excessive questions, field support is notified so that the franchisee can be coached on her selection or training of her staff members. Sometimes a franchisee becomes dependent on turning to the support center for everything, and field support needs to address cutting the cord. They might suggest that the franchisee have one of his staff members attend training again or hire another team member, or we might implement a plan to charge per call above a certain number to recover our costs.

One of the side benefits of having the support center for the franchisees who handle the sales role is that it allows them to remain out in the field, making sales calls instead of getting sucked back into the office by their branch personnel. The support center provides a safety net in the beginning for the franchisee's branch team by walking the team through processing payroll, billing clients, placing a recruiting ad, etc. The key to success for this extra layer of support is to establish the support center as a bridge to building competency so that the franchisee's team becomes self-sufficient in a reasonable period of time—normally within three months.

The average cost of the team is far less than for BrightStart or field support because the background needed does not require extensive sales or leadership experience. It is, however, a great area for team members looking for advancement to build general knowledge of the system.

Field Support

The field support team is commonly the lifeblood of a franchise system, because it is the team closest to the franchisees and is responsible for working with the franchisees to improve their businesses and to set goals. Typically, a normal job description for field support includes an overwhelming array of expectations of leadership, operations, sales, and financial acumen. Over the years, however, I've learned that the most critical skills needed in field support personnel are leadership, the ability to establish mutual respect and trust with the franchisees, and the ability to have difficult conversations with franchisees.

We have found it is much more cost-effective to direct questions and small requests to the support center so that the field support team is available to review a franchisee's operation and work with her on an action plan to achieve her goals. With the addition of BrightStart, we no longer had to seek strong sales acumen in our field support. We hire members for the field support team who focus strategically on performance improvement initiatives, enabling our franchisees (and us) to achieve breakthrough performance and to grow into future brands. We provide the resources for field support to call upon such as BrightStart as the sales SME or the franchisee financial services director (discussed below) as the financial SME to enable the field support director to be the primary party accountable to maximize franchisee performance, leveraging the skills and services of others.

But we still had a need for field support to have strong financial acumen. In a tight credit market, there is a growing need to help franchisees access the capital they need to grow and to understand the financial impact of pricing and hiring on their cash flow and profitability. This requirement was difficult to find in every field support person, so we originally searched for either candidates who were generalists with modest skills in a variety of areas, such as operations and finance, or candidates who were strong in operations and leadership but did not have the financial acumen to support franchisees. This need for financial acumen and capital access support caused us to identify how much more efficient field support could be if the field support director had a resource to engage to help franchisees with finance-specific needs.

Fortunately, my senior vice president of operations at the time identified the need for a dedicated franchisee financial services director (FFSD). This position would help franchisees meet their needs and tighten the hiring protocol for the field support team. This position has been one of our best additions in years.

Because many franchisees do not have financial acumen, providing them with the FFSD-developed financial training sessions takes on significant relevance. The sessions show them how to set goals, understand the cash flow impact of the decisions they make, and calculate and understand their breakeven. In addition, the FFSD meets one-on-one with each franchisee to assess the franchisee's cash flow, breakeven, and needs for accessing capital. The FFSD reviews the financial position of each franchisee periodically and serves as the primary conduit to accessing outside capital programs.

Our field support team refers all franchisee cash flow and capital access issues directly to the FFSD. The franchise sales team, as needed, can also seek help from the FFSD. We found that it was helpful to have someone in this role who understood operations from the financial metrics and cash flow standpoint. We also discovered that former bankers had the ideal experience to fill this role. They understand what the banks are looking for, and they can be an effective intermediary between the banks and the franchisee in seeking (and accessing) capital.

Our last breakthrough was the addition of facilitated performance groups for franchisees at similar stages (years in business, multi-unit, etc.). I learned about this from the great senior team at PostNet, and we floated the idea by some of our franchisees (those beyond two years in business) to see if they would prefer this type of support in lieu of a field support visit. In every case, the franchisees found that this would be a great enhancement, and they were eager to trade their normal one-on-one support visit with a facilitated group interaction with their peers to share best practices. These types of sessions were also the most attended and highest rated sessions at our annual franchisee conference.

Likewise, technology can play a major part in simplifying the franchisee on-boarding process as well as enabling the franchisees to share information, access information, and collaborate in a "community." The next section describes how best to use technology solutions to simplify the on-boarding and support processes for your franchisees.

Technology Options to Simplify On-boarding and Support Processes

We discussed in the earlier sections of this chapter the processes that need to be in place and the resources necessary to successfully on-board and support franchisees. Technology can assist in automating and/or streamlining these processes. However, there are trade-offs between cost and capability that must be considered.

Since you don't know how many franchisees you will have when you launch a franchise, you will need to make a big decision between selecting a franchise support system that can be implemented for under $5,000 per year and one that costs up to 10 times that amount. The ideal solution is to find technology that is built on a sophisticated technology platform that will meet your needs for the long term. The trick is to find the vendor willing to partner with you to provide this type of technology platform at a reasonable per-user price, so that the cost corresponds with the size of your system as it grows. We used an inexpensive system for our first three years (and first 100 franchise units) that was a solid system for what we needed at the time.

As we grew and wanted to integrate capabilities with our core system, it was apparent that we needed more. We wanted to build a multiyear road map for the technologies we would use to (1) track support with solid communication across all support departments, through to the last contact with a franchisee; (2) on-board franchisees and track where they were in the preopening process; and (3) provide franchisee access to all information and resources through easy searches and enable franchisee-to-franchisee collaboration. During the transition period, we tried out tools that did not require a long-term commitment, allowing us to evaluate the capabilities we needed. We were investing in getting all of our technology pieces to "talk" with one another, and we found that technologies outside the franchise space aligned better with this goal. We moved our collaboration spaces and LMS to a WebEx tool, which documented and consolidated all of our information into one place to prepare us for the migration to SharePoint.

Franchise-specific technologies are used by some franchisors. These technologies provide the tools for tracking franchisee support and allow franchisees to collaborate. We made the decision to invest in SharePoint (once we had nearly 200 franchise units sold) for (1) warehousing all resources, including operations manuals, since the whole site is searchable; (2) enabling franchisee collaboration with other franchisees; (3) extracting key information to populate dashboards for our franchisees as to their performance; and (4) automating and/or streamlining end-to-end processes, from franchise sales to on-boarding franchisees to supporting them after they are open. This is a strong addition to our system and aligns with our vision for all of our technology to be integrated, enabling us to eliminate data entry duplication, achieve better reporting, and streamline process flows. When the technology is easy to use and has a consistent look and feel and functionality, it is easier for franchisees to learn and ramp up.

BRIGHT IDEA:

The selection of technology for on-boarding and supporting franchisees is an important one. You need to balance initial cost, recurring cost, and the underlying technology platform that the systems are built on.

I recommend that you allocate the resources necessary to do it right in the beginning or as soon as you are financially able.

Closing Thoughts

The on-boarding and training of franchisees and the support of franchisees over time are critical components in the success of a system. The lessons shared in this chapter have been my greatest breakthroughs in improving revenues, year over year. On-boarding and training franchisees so that they can open fully prepared to grow their businesses quickly will maximize the franchisor's revenues. Developing an organizational structure for the support team allows employees to be hired with the specialized skills needed without their having to be great at everything (which is unrealistic). Our organizational structure allows BrightStart to be focused on sales, the support center to be focused on administrative needs, the field support team to be focused on leadership and operations, and the FFSD to be focused on financial acumen, all coordinated by field support to ensure one group has the ability to drive franchisee performance by leveraging others but also so one group has clear accountability for results. This allows us to hire the right people for the right positions and pay, based upon the primary skills we need. Technology can enable greater scale and efficiency to the on-boarding and support process as well.

·   ·   ·

So far in this section we have discussed the programs and tactics to drive franchisee performance and in turn maximize franchisor royalties. In the next chapter, we discuss how large an impact culture has on achieving the desired results from these programs and tactics. It is not enough for me, as CEO, to focus on how to continuously improve franchisee results; my entire organization must be aligned with the same mission and be able to see the vision for the brand and how each person fits into and enables it. Likewise, franchisees must be selected for their culture fit.

CHAPTER 10

After the Launch: An Intentional Culture

Every organization has a culture. Frequently in business, a culture is developed unintentionally, as employees watch the actions of the leader and see which activities are rewarded and which are not. I believe the best cultures are intentionally built. But building an intentional culture takes work: The leader must be focused on sharing the vision of where the organization is going, how the organization will get there, and what role each employee plays in the journey. Ensuring that the culture stays pure means hiring for attitude that fits the culture and parting ways with employees who do not fit the culture.

The BrightStar Culture

The culture of BrightStar is based upon open communication, a results orientation, and high energy and passion for making a difference in the lives of other employees, in the lives of our franchisees, and in the lives of the customers and employees our franchisees support on the front line. I believe wholeheartedly that for me to succeed, my franchisees must succeed. Likewise, I want franchisees who also want the franchisor to be profitable and successful as long as they themselves are.

Let me share a story from one of our quarterly all-system calls, which we call our "Town Hall." We encourage franchisees to submit questions through an anonymous survey tool prior to our Town Hall call. One of the questions that recently came in was, "Will you be using *our* royalties to launch these future brands that you are talking about?" There was probably a system-wide and corporate-wide inhaling of breath when I read the question aloud and prepared my answer.

This is what I said.

> As the sole owner of the franchise company, I could distribute profits and buy a big house *or* I could reinvest in the company, building new companies that could benefit our employees' and franchisees' future opportunities. The royalties that we receive are part of our earnings formula for which we have invested for years. *We* lost money for several years because of the investments we made in support of our franchisees far above industry ratios. We are in business to make money, too, as this is not a not-for-profit venture. Much like how your customers pay you contributes to your profits and your customers don't ask how their monies are spent, we receive money from our franchisees for the licensing of our brand, systems, and for the support we provide.

It was a direct answer to a sensitive topic. The chat board lit up like a Christmas tree, with messages from many, many franchisees saying things like "Go, Shelly!" "You tell them!" "Go, girl!"

I started with this story because becoming a franchisor has sometimes been a struggle for me between following my heart and following my head. I want to give as much as possible to the franchisees to align with what is in my heart, and I worry that some franchisees question why I don't invest every last dime on support. The franchisor must be financially sound and profitable for the brand to be resilient for the long term. And the franchisor must balance this need to be profitable with spending to ensure the franchisees have the tools and resources available to help replicate the business model. With the right heart and the right intentions—to enable the potential for a franchisee to be successful—the right tactics can be implemented to facilitate strong communication and to enable increased franchisee satisfaction over time. A franchisor enables the potential for franchisee success through a solid business model with branding, systems, and various areas of support. The franchisee adds his capital, commitment, and hard work to determine his own success in using the business model.

ESTABLISHING AN INTENTIONAL CULTURE

How does one set out to build an intentional culture? Well, I think culture begins with heart and builds from there. If in the beginning the culture is unintentional, that is, based on the heart of the senior leadership team who know that their success is dependent upon franchisee success, the goal over time should be to make this belief and commitment intentional through specific communication of the mission of the organization, so that it permeates the entire organization.

If a strong intentional culture of shared success is the goal, how do you go about creating it? The corporate team must see that you and your senior leadership team are committed to franchisees' success and to the continuous improvement of franchisees' unit economics. It is important to have equal weighting annually as part of your strategic planning and budgeting process to maximize franchisor profitability *and* to maximize franchisee profitability. Then, you should focus on building this accountability into job descriptions, performance reviews, and bonus programs. To maximize both franchisor and franchisee profitability, there must be a culture in which new ideas, suggestions for improvement, and best practices are freely shared among all constituencies—franchisees with corporate, corporate with franchisees, and franchisees with one another.

Our corporate values, which we discuss regularly with employees, include one that is directly related to this discussion: shared success. What does shared success mean to BrightStar? Shared success requires active listening to franchisees with different backgrounds when they make suggestions for improvement or share what is working locally in their market. We have created a culture in which franchisees have a voice and an opportunity to expand their revenue sources in their market. That makes them want to collaborate with corporate to share their ideas, gain feedback, and, if the idea is successful, ultimately obtain new marketing materials to make potential customers aware of the new service.

In addition to active listening to include franchisees in the continuous improvement of the brand, we must also focus on franchisee unit economics. I recognize that I will maintain strong relationships with my franchisees only if they have the opportunity to be financially successful at a reasonable point in time (so long as they follow the business model, are in the business for the right reasons, and are giving the business their all). We set out to have a work-hard, play-hard culture that delivers results. We constantly challenge ourselves to improve franchisee revenue levels and gross margins, to optimize franchisee processes for efficiency and scalability, and to reduce the costs of items that franchisees purchase from our suppliers. If the franchisees can see our commitment to these things and a constant improvement in each area, then relationships stay strong. And strong franchisee–franchisor relationships are key to a positive, mutually beneficial, and sustainable culture.

We made a strong culture possible by encouraging open communication, soliciting franchisee feedback, establishing a Franchise Advisory Council, and recognizing the achievements of franchisees in performance *and* participation. Our intended culture was built upon a set of core principles—to create a model built upon shared success, in which everybody wins (and demonstrating our understanding that, if franchisees win, then we win); to create an atmosphere where we work hard and play hard and have fun; and to create a healthy environment with open collaboration and sharing of information and feedback. I have seen that providing open access to information, so franchisees can see one another's performance and what is possible, fosters a very team-oriented culture where franchisees reach out to the top performers for help on how to improve. Franchisees will believe they can improve, which is half the battle, when they see what others are accomplishing. Franchisees also need forums in which to share information with corporate and with one another.

OPEN COMMUNICATION

We have built a culture with open communication: in numbers, in sharing best practices, and in sharing priorities and initiatives. At BrightStar, our franchisees have protected territories, so they are not competing with one another. Therefore, we believe that enabling franchisees to see one another's key metrics, such as revenues, gross margin, mix of business, etc., allows them to see what is possible and to seek best practices. In the beginning we allowed all franchisees to opt in to this information-sharing process, and if anyone did not want her information shared she didn't have to participate. When two franchisees chose to opt out of sharing their information, I reminded them that they would then be denied access to the system's numbers. Both conceded that if the only way to get that information was to participate, they would participate. We no longer offer franchisees the option to opt out. We want all prospects to understand before they join that open access is part of our culture and we will not make exceptions for individual franchisees.

Because I also have been a franchisee, I understand how lonely it can be.

I constantly asked myself questions such as these: "Am I on track?" "How do I compare to my peers?" "Who can I call when I need to speak with someone who has had a similar experience?" I wanted my franchisees to be able to compare their performance with the performances of others who had been open a similar period of time. I wanted my franchisees to know how they were performing locally, regionally, and nationally on sales and margins. I wanted to open the doors of communication so that a franchisee who was above average on sales dollars but below average on gross margin percentage would be able to identify a franchisee who was below average on sales dollars but above average on gross margin percentage. They could then share their best practices to help each other improve. This is exactly what has happened.

When I ask prospects what surprised them when they made validation calls to franchisees, I am told over and over again that our franchisees were smart, very engaged, knew other franchisees very well, knew their numbers and how they compared across the system, and generally seemed like one big family. This is probably the greatest compliment that I hear from prospects.

We started slow, initially sharing only revenue ranking, and then we worked with our Franchise Advisory Council (which I describe in more detail later in this chapter) to identify the other key metrics they felt would be helpful for franchisees to know. Automating the gathering of information is critical to enabling this aspect of a culture, but it doesn't happen overnight. Nearly three years after we decided to gather the information, we are still working to fully integrate financial statements and accounts receivable information into the dashboards and reporting tools that our franchisees access.

Similar to how a business needs a strategic plan, a human resources (talent) plan, a marketing plan, and a technology plan, a business intelligence plan should also be in place. This plan should map out what investments will be needed over time to aggregate all pertinent information from internal and external sources, which will enable franchisees to have easier access to information so that they can make better and faster decisions to improve their business.

BRIGHT IDEA:

As you begin to plan for how to eventually enable open access to information, you will want to think about how to get key information on one common technology platform, as BrightStar has done with our investment in SharePoint, so the information is available to facilitate reporting.

BEST PRACTICES CALLS

You can see we have built intentional processes and feedback loops to drive open communication across our system. With open access to information as a way to show all franchisees what is possible and who among them is knocking the ball out of the park on particular metrics, we also host monthly regional best practices calls to allow a structured way for franchisees to share what is working for them. The corporate host shares updates and improvements during the first five to 10 minutes. The host then introduces a preidentified specific franchisee to share for about 15 minutes a best practices tip for driving increased business. The remainder of the hour is an open forum for franchisees to share with or ask questions of one another.

Franchisees like to learn from one another. The reality is that franchisees will listen to one another more than they will listen to corporate. Conference calls are easy to set up because the regional field support directors will be aware of who is succeeding in their region and of the interesting niche opportunities franchisees are uncovering that will be worthwhile to share with others. The key is to make sure that time is dedicated to this great initiative.

SYSTEM-WIDE COMMUNICATION

In addition to these targeted best practices calls, we emphasize frequent system-wide communication to keep franchisees informed about the future direction of the system and the investments under way that will improve their results. Like most organizations, we distribute a newsletter that contains short updates. We e-mailed the newsletters until we realized that new owners would be able to ramp up more easily if they had access to our entire archive (and could search to find topics of interest). We moved to a system that hosted the newsletter, but the system required a password to log on, which created another barrier to maximizing the effectiveness of this type of communication. Investing in SharePoint has enabled us to communicate in a newsletter format, archive the newsletters, make the content fully searchable, and provide the franchisee with easy access.

Our experience with our newsletter illustrates how difficult it is for a franchisor to get everything right the first time. But if franchisors are intentional about creating a culture in which there is open, constructive communication so that the franchisees and the franchisor alike can continually improve the system, improve communications, and improve one another's results, then the right solutions will come over time.

As I mentioned in the story at the beginning of this chapter, we also host a formal system-wide conference call four times a year that we call our Town Hall. Prior to the call, we invite franchisees to anonymously submit any questions they may have so that we can update the system on the most popular topics while providing a venue in which franchisees can have their questions answered by the appropriate senior staff member. Each of our senior staff provides an update of the past three months regarding improvement, what is currently in process, and what is targeted for the next three to six months. This information helps paint a picture of how we are constantly striving to do three things for our franchisees: (1) increase revenues, (2) reduce costs, and/or (3) enable efficiency or better information for scalability. The percentage of the presubmitted questions answered by the senior staff's presentations indicates how aligned we are in our efforts to meet franchisees' needs. Anything that was not answered or addressed by the presentation is answered specifically at the end of the call.

You really cannot communicate too much. I have learned that it takes about five times to communicate a system change before it sinks in. Build in multiple forums for communicating to franchisees. The Town Hall format is a great way to move the conversation away from the tactical day-to-day (those issues are covered by most other communication methods) to the innovative changes that are coming. It is critical to prepare a system for change before it actually occurs, and having a preset quarterly call scheduled to discuss this type of information helps to prepare the system for the continuous improvement component of our system and our culture.

Anonymous Surveys of Franchisees

We anonymously survey our franchisees twice a year across such key areas as initial training, ongoing support, marketing programs, resources, etc., to determine how we are performing and what our performance trend is over time. Our anonymous surveys also ask open-ended questions about the franchisor and/or the system, including the following three critical ones: (1) What do you like best? (2) What suggestions do you have for improvement? (3) What concerns do you have?

As I discuss in chapter 7, we use both of the franchise industry survey leaders annually, one every six months. In early January we use FBR in time for the FBR rankings used in the marketing programs of Franchise 50, a recognition and lead-generation effort sponsored for their clients who receive strong scores from their franchisees. Approximately six months later we go through the process again with FranSurvey. The FBR and FranSurvey information has been invaluable in assisting us with prioritizing what is important to franchisees as well as informing us about what issues franchisees are concerned about so we can communicate again and again on these issues to alleviate franchisee anxiety.

The founder of FranSurvey, Jeff Johnson, is great about scheduling a call with us to go over the results when the reports are ready. A former franchisee himself, he understands franchisees' needs and is a huge franchisee advocate. But he also is very fair in helping franchisors understand the reality of the bell-shaped curve. FranSurvey gives participants a pass-or-fail grade: If 67 percent of your system is satisfied across a key set of questions, you are "certified"; if more than 33 percent is unsatisfied, you are not certified. We have worked hard to have scores in the 80s and above across the years. Being a perfectionist who has a big heart and wants every franchisee to succeed and be happy, my heart sank the first time I reviewed the report. I was used to being an A student, and I didn't see a 100 percent satisfaction in many places. Jeff helped me get perspective: I should consider receiving above 67 percent as successful, and scores in the 80s as remarkable for a new franchisor. He also reminded me that it is impossible to please everyone. He emphasized the importance of reading the open-ended answers, communicating the survey results openly with the system, and directionally working to improve the lowest areas over time. That is what we have done, and it was good advice.

We have built the review of the survey results into a formal process. I tend to want to fix everything, but I have learned—with the help of a great group of employees and franchisees—that it is better to fix the top 10 problems at 100 percent than fix a greater number at less than 100 percent.

A key member of my senior team takes the write-in results from the suggestions for improvement and areas of concern questions and categorizes them by themes. For us the themes may be unique, such as licensure/regulation, national accounts, business mix, technology upgrades, financial systems, searchable resources, etc. The themes then receive a number for the number of times the theme was mentioned in the responses to these two questions. This list is then sorted from highest to lowest number, and the top 10 are prioritized with an action plan of projects and/or initiatives that can improve the results in the next three to nine months. This list is then shared with the Franchise Advisory Council to validate the priorities and to obtain their participation as we work in the upcoming months to drive improvement.

I mentioned above my knee-jerk impulse to fix all of the items that franchisees provide feedback on. I always want to say "yes," but have realized that, over the past few years, the times I said "no" or "not now" were the best decisions I made for the benefit of the brand and the system over the long term. Staying true to the brand positioning and differentiators is absolutely the right course.

As you launch your franchise system, obtaining information from your franchisees is critical for continuous improvement and for prioritizing the improvements needed. Surveys are a high-value, low-cost method to allow franchisees to have a strong voice in letting you know how you are doing, what needs to be improved, and what to be cautious of. Obtaining survey information from franchisees regularly allows you to have the confidence in moving forward because you are aware of what you are doing well and what areas need improvement. Diligently focusing on franchisee feedback allows you to proactively address any potential negative issues that could harm you as franchisees talk to prospects during the validation phase.

BRIGHT IDEA:

The time you spend to publish the survey results, to review the feedback, and to prioritize an action plan will pay dividends in three critical ways—franchisee satisfaction, improved system results, and improved franchisee validation.

Franchise Advisory Council

All of the forums of two-way, system-wide communication are indispensable in building an open, engaged culture. In addition, it is extremely helpful to have a group of trusted franchisees to use as a sounding board for new ideas and initiatives and to make the corporate team aware of issues that we should be focused on. At a certain stage of growth, a franchisor will normally establish a Franchise Advisory Council (FAC) to provide this type of resource. The International Franchise Association (IFA) website (www.franchise.org) offers excellent advice about forming an FAC. Instead of repeating what you can learn there, I will share my experience and point out what I would have done differently.

The IFA tools for establishing an FAC are great when applied to systems above 100 to 200 units, but they may need to be modified for a smaller system. In a brand-new system, franchisees are also new, which means they are focused on building their business and covering payroll. Knowing now what I didn't know then, I would start with a more informal group of two or three as part of a President's Council and work up from there. On reaching 50 franchisees, I'd have done better to establish the more formal FAC but limit the elections to those franchisees in compliance with brand standards, with more than 18 months' experience, and with the requisite infrastructure. That way, I would have just six franchisees on the FAC until we reached 100 to 150 franchisees, at which time I would expand the group to 12 members.

AVOID THIS PITFALL:

If I could do it over, I would first identify the franchisees who had built enough of an infrastructure to be able to commit the time to this activity and only invite those franchisees that had the bandwidth to participate on the FAC—even if this meant forming the FAC with a smaller group of franchisees.

An FAC can be exceedingly helpful when employed strategically. For the first couple of years, I informed our FAC of major new initiatives and waited for their input before rolling the initiatives out to the entire system. The council also helped provide feedback and input as to tactical issues of concern to them or their fellow franchisees. In late 2009 (after four years of franchising), however, we had a breakthrough in our system when we moved the conversations with our FAC to a more strategic level—sharing our vision of the future without already having the action plans for realizing the vision. We then worked with them to prioritize the list of 12 projects (given resource constraint parameters) they had identified, narrowing it down to the five or six with the highest ROI for the franchisees. Together, the corporate team and the FAC communicated to the entire system the priorities for the upcoming year and stayed true to what we had agreed were the critical initiatives.

Your takeaway is that there is no one-size-fits-all approach to forming an FAC. In your initial stage of franchising, an informal structure with a couple of franchisees to leverage as a sounding board will be much more effective and simpler to implement than a full-blown FAC. You then can evolve the number of representatives and the strategic nature of the conversation as you evolve the franchise system. As the franchisor, you will be the decision maker, but you do want the valuable input, buy-in, and leadership of an FAC.

Recognition

Often a franchisee is willing to talk about issues with a fellow franchisee, and the Franchise Advisory Council provides the vehicle to do this. Franchisees also want to be recognized among their peers. We have quarterly award programs that publicly (via e-mail) recognize franchisees for reaching new business milestones. A franchisee who reaches a new level of billable hours in a quarter receives a plaque to hang in his office. We make the final night of our annual conferences a night of celebration in which we recognize top performers—among our franchisees' teams at the Branch Leadership Conference and among our franchisees at the Franchisee Conference. In addition to the public recognition at the conferences, the award winners receive plaques for their offices to commemorate their accomplishments.

We also have a President's Circle group that recognizes the top performing franchisees in the system, and this group is recognized with an amazing incentive trip. Thanks to some great advice from Dave McKinnon, founder of Service Brands, we have made the year-over-year dollar increase a major focus so that newer franchisees have an opportunity to attend. We have also limited the number we recognize to the top 4 percent of franchisees or to 10 franchisees, whichever is smaller. We award one spot with the top revenue-producing office, we award a second spot with the top revenue-producing multi-unit owner, and all other spots are for the franchisees with the highest year-over-year increase in revenue dollars. Limiting the trips to a group of no more than 10 franchisees with their partners, the brand president, and J.D. and me makes it more special and intimate for everyone.

We didn't start offering incentive trips until 2010—but once we were able to afford this recognition we added it. We wanted them to be recognized for their achievements as the best in the system, and they and their partners were rewarded with a trip to a five-star resort with first-class airfare, so the franchisees feel truly pampered and appreciated.

Recognition doesn't have to cost anything. In the early stages, public e-mails are free and are a proven motivator of franchisees. As the system grows and money can be allocated to recognition programs, I recommend that you make this investment. Recognition drives and often increases levels of performance. I believe the investment pays for itself many times over.

Additional Suggestions

You should recognize that franchisees will develop their own collective culture for their organization. It is important to create a framework in terms of the vision, mission, and values the brand stands for so that there is consistency in the heart and passion behind the brand in every market around the world. We provide franchisee staff with on-boarding and orientation materials, including videos, to ensure that the message of what BrightStar stands for remains strong and consistent. With a strong foundation, franchisees will build their own local culture around their work style, energy level, etc.

In addition to the ways of building an intentional culture outlined in this chapter, there are a few other observations from BrightStar's history that have impacted our relationship with our franchisees—both in terms of trust and accountability. The areas that had the most impact relate to voluntary changes to the franchise agreement, to franchisee conferences, and to the communication of new programs. (These circumstances may never happen to you, but in case they do, you'll learn the valuable lessons prior to embarking on the specific situation described.)

During the recession of 2008 and 2009, we voluntarily reduced performance requirements for franchisees on their initial locations (low enough to ensure that the majority of actual average and median levels for compliant franchisees were higher than the minimums) and suspended minimum performance requirements on additional locations for our multi-unit owners. This means that although we had a contractual right to collect minimum performance royalties, we chose to abate the financial opportunity for ourselves and have franchisees invest their money in themselves as long as they were following the model. We felt that if they were doing their best—following the model—and couldn't achieve certain levels of performance that the majority of franchisees achieved before the recession, we would do our part to ride out the economy with them, with all of us suffering a little. We also invested in the BrightStart and boost programs so that we could all enter 2010 stronger.

We communicated the concessions early to reduce franchisee stress. At the same time, we communicated that with the BrightStart investments made in increased head count, increased travel, and increased technology, we would need to restart minimums on additional locations at the beginning of 2010 as though it were day one for these locations, and that first locations would be accountable for minimum performance levels once again. We offered to work with franchisees who could not access capital to open their additional locations to provide an opportunity for them to sell these locations (many could be sold for much more than the franchisees paid for them).

We also sought opportunities to create a win-win for franchisees and for us. When we began looking at international expansion (which we will discuss further in chapter 13), we wanted to create an opportunity to share this exciting opportunity with our franchisees. Knowing that the sale of a master franchise would bring in an up-front cash infusion, we communicated to the system that once we sold our second master we would voluntarily change the royalty payment terms for our older franchisees to the current standard and create a two-week royalty holiday for improved cash flows (the original contract remittance was 15 days and had evolved to 28 days). When we signed our second master in December 2010, many franchisees got to celebrate their temporary cash flow improvement. Even those newer franchisees that already had the longer remittance term were positive about the change; they expressed how rare it was for someone to voluntarily make a change that pushed 101 percent of the cash flow benefit of the second master fees back out to the franchisees.

The message is that we let external factors and a desire to do the right thing dictate terms that were different—and more favorable to the franchisees—from what was in the franchise agreement. At the same time, we were clear as to how long this would last and what the expectations would be after this period of time. I would love to say that every franchisee used the time and concessions to get their houses in order, but at the end of 2010 a few were still surprised by the change in expectations. That said, generally all franchisees recognize and communicate that we are fair and that they know we are aligned on the importance of a win-win relationship. Of course we are. Franchisees must win for the franchisor to win.

Franchisee conferences are a great way to collaborate, share best practices, and get everyone aligned and focused on winning together. It is probably obvious that franchisee conferences are an efficient way to share information. The benefits of getting everyone together go far beyond this; every attendee leaves energized and renewed, and ready to go make things happen.

BRIGHT IDEA:

It will serve you and your franchisees well if you set a requirement in your franchise disclosure document that all franchisees must attend the annual conference.

Making attendance mandatory was one of the best pieces of advice I received early on, and if a franchisee couldn't attend she would still pay the registration fee (to cover your budget related to room and meeting space forecasts).

The second part of the advice that I received related to franchisee conferences was to actually charge a registration fee! A fitness franchisor who had never charged franchisees for attending the conference initiated a $300 hospitality fee one year, whereupon the whole system revolted. As a franchisee in two hotels, I know that registration fees in the hospitality industry commonly cost about $1,000 or more per person. If the conferences are great—with good content, networking, and entertainment—the registration fee is justified. Learning from the fitness franchisor's misstep and attending the hotel franchise conferences made it easy for me to decide to establish a registration fee from the beginning and disclose it as required in our FDD.

The conference is not a moneymaker. In addition to all the time the staff spends working on it, we still financially contribute over and above the registration fees and exhibitor fees collected. Building the registration fee expectation allows us to put on a better event with a higher ROI for our franchisees. The greatest cost to the franchisees is the time away from their business and their travel costs, so a registration fee to guarantee that the event is worthwhile is a small price to pay in the big scheme of things. I also believe that by having to pay a registration fee, the franchisees come to the conference with the expectation of getting more value for the cost and are more engaged in the learning and networking to ensure that it happens.

I wish I could get a do-over of our 2009 Franchisee Conference. I explained two of the large investments we had made to improve our system—BrightStart and an online learning management system—to the room full of franchisees. These initiatives would help new (or future) franchisees, so our franchisees who had already invested with us pointed out that the programs wouldn't help *them* with their businesses. In my five years of leading the organization, it was my biggest miss, and the months following were my hardest time in our professional history. Our franchisees felt from my speech that I had lost touch and was more focused on adding new franchisees than on supporting *them*. This couldn't have been further from the truth, but I needed to show them. I engaged our employees and our Franchise Advisory Council to help me.

AVOID THIS PITFALL:

One of the hardest and biggest lessons learned was that the way new programs are launched—and, more important, how they are communicated—can greatly impact the culture.

I knew we had already spent a lot on the employee additions and on the technology for BrightStart, so I needed to figure out how these programs could help existing franchisees too. This led to the boost program described earlier. Likewise, I knew that the online learning management system was built to help new franchisees hit the ground running faster and to ensure that all classroom attendees were at a similar learning level, regardless of background, before attending. The investment had been made in the content development and the technology, so how could it be repurposed to help existing franchisees? We quickly saw that helping established franchisees use the training would benefit them. It would work to assure them that their team was up to date on new programs and to help when they added or replaced team members. Again, the investment was 99 percent there, so we worked to add access and to split the curriculum by role; we also added content that would specifically help existing franchisees. Within six months of the September 2009 conference misstep, we were back on a well-aligned plan forward, with key initiatives benefiting all franchisees. This experience taught me a huge lesson.

BRIGHT IDEA:

Stay conscious of ways to adapt new programs to assist both new *and existing* franchisees—it doesn't cost appreciably more, and the benefits to the culture are huge.

Closing Thoughts

Most cultures evolve over time unintentionally, and the end result may not be desired. You now have a road map of items to consider in forming a strong culture with your franchisees based on open access to information and strong communication. Showing franchisees that corporate is committed to their success and to listening to their input builds a strong win-win culture. In addition, when franchisees see strong ongoing corporate commitment to the franchisees' results, then the culture is collaborative. If all of your communication venues—including surveys, best practices calls, the Franchise Advisory Council, and recognition programs—are at least partially about improving franchisees' unit economics, then you have probably anchored your system in a positive and intentional culture.

. . .

We talked about how the best intentional culture aligns the win-win, shared success for franchisor and franchisees, recognizing that the positive effects of successful and happy franchisees are contagious. In the next chapter, we will focus on how to specifically improve a franchisee's unit economics—one of the key elements in keeping your franchisees successful and happy.

CHAPTER 11

Relentless Pursuit of Improving and Sustaining Franchisee Unit Economics

The previous chapter was about building an intentional culture centered on the premise of win-win and collaboration. Let's now discuss the philosophical and cultural norms that must exist to maximize the outcomes in improving franchisee unit economics. The health of the entire franchise system is essentially based on continuous improvement in two metrics: unit-level economics (at the franchisee and franchisor levels) and franchisee satisfaction. Each is a relentless pursuit.

First you must incent the right behavior for corporate personnel. In chapter 4, we discussed the design of our quarterly bonus program. We review projects and initiatives to ensure that they are driving improvement for franchisees in the following four areas: revenues, margin, costs, and efficiency. Some departments, such as field support and BrightStart, may have a greater opportunity to impact revenues, while another, such as national accounts, may have a greater opportunity to impact margins (I discuss this later in the chapter). Having our senior leadership team collectively review the quarterly goals for each employee enables us to monitor and assure that progress is being made for the franchisees across all areas.

The next philosophical belief is not for the faint of heart: You must constantly evaluate a franchisor-franchisee scorecard and challenge yourself, as the franchisor, to look for ways to deliver more in value to the franchisee than you receive in payments from the franchisee. Having begun as a franchisee, I recognize that a common problem within the franchisee–franchisor relationship is that the franchisee pays an initial franchise fee to learn the business model, license the marks, and receive initial support, but two or three years into the relationship the franchisee forgets the initial support he received and begins to wonder, "What have you done for me lately?" In other words, he begins to question the ROI on the royalties he pays.

True, the franchisor is entitled under the contract to the royalties, and the franchisee acquires great value in being able to use the trademarks, systems, and processes that the franchisor spent lots of money developing and maintaining. However, one measure that I believe deserves consideration from time to time is this: In the aggregate, for franchisees who are following the system and executing on all that is expected of them, shouldn't the royalties paid be buying quantifiable value, if they are leveraging all the tools we have developed for their use? In fact, the gross margins on business that we bring to franchisees (through national accounts and surge programs), as well as the discounts on products and services the franchisees buy through approved vendors, need to contribute more to their bottom line, on average, than what they pay in royalties. There should never be any question about whether being a franchisee is better than being independent, provided the franchisee has followed the system, played by the rules, and given everything he has in being part of the team. I believe this also ensures a higher likelihood of renewals when the 10-year mark (or whatever your renewal period will be) comes around.

We won't balance the scorecard in the franchisee's favor for every franchisee, but that is our goal, and it is a measure that we are beginning to look at more closely as our system matures. We haven't reached our first renewal, but I want to drive our accountability to ensure that, by the time our franchisees start renewing, all of them will know unequivocally that renewal is in their best interest. This also allows me to set the expectation of and empower the various teams to achieve this result—or at least closing any imbalance and moving in the right direction until renewal. This also is the ultimate scorecard that we can review on an exception basis as an organization to know which franchisees we need to focus on and to investigate the root cause if franchisees are not taking advantage of the resources we make available to balance the scorecard.

Keys to Improving Franchisee Unit Economics

Now that we have discussed BrightStar's philosophical guidelines and how we integrate them into setting the vision for our culture, let's begin to look at improving franchisee unit economics. There is no better way to ensure strong relationships with franchisees and a strong financial model for the franchisor than to have all the right people in the franchisor organization focused on improving franchisee unit economics. There should be a relentless pursuit of constantly improving in at least one, and preferably all, of four key areas: (1) increase franchisee revenues, (2) improve franchisee gross margins, (3) reduce franchisee expenditures on products and services, and (4) improve franchisee efficiency to increase their revenues-per-dollar-of-payroll (for us, this is just for office staff since our field healthcare employee costs are included in cost of goods sold). The following sections describe what we are doing and what future investments we are making to impact each of these four areas.

Increase Revenues

There is no single silver bullet to increase top-line revenues. A multi-pronged approach is needed to help franchisees acquire new customers, retain existing customers, and sell more to existing customers. The key to overall success in improving franchisee revenues is to guarantee that there is an absolute focus and commitment to the effort, starting from the top of the organization and reaching every level, and then ensuring that each initiative has measurable goals so that improvement can be documented and communicated to franchisees. Being able to communicate to franchisees the positive impact of these efforts in quantitative terms goes a long way toward maintaining high franchisee satisfaction while simultaneously improving franchisee unit economics.

Our goals to reach more customers include the implementation of online strategies and investments in our website, search engine optimization (SEO), search engine marketing (SEM), and social media. We track the increase in visitors month by month and the cost of new leads; we also compare the cost of the leads and the average amount spent by a new customer to document our franchisees' ROI on their national advertising fund dollars. We track closely what our customers are saying about us with online reputation management tools. We have implemented tools and provided the incremental resources for our franchisees to build out their own web pages as part of our brand domain, and have trained and supported their use of social media tools such as LinkedIn, Twitter, Facebook, and blogs to build their local awareness. We made a great decision in hiring someone fresh out of school with a marketing degree and passion and interest in social media. We turned her loose, and she amazed us and our franchisees with what she was able to deliver.

National online referral sources must also continually be evaluated. It seems as though a new one pops up every week, so it is important to have your online expert perform due diligence on these sites to see how good their traffic and results are. Often it is better to have franchisees spend more on SEM that is directed to their own website page, within our main domain, than to build the awareness of another site. We try to keep a handle on the sites that appear to have a solid ROI and provide that information to franchisees for them to consider advertising, but also make them aware of where their money will likely not be a wise investment.

Online presence can help new potential customers become aware of your brand. This is a critical priority and will only increase in the future as busy customers initiate more decisions and transactions online. In addition to increasing the number of customers who are aware of our brand through marketing, we also need to constantly assist our franchisees with new sales programs, marketing programs, etc., to gain more customers. We have a couple of initiatives that we work on to do this (some are more unique to our industry, but by dedicating time to thinking about similar initiatives applicable to your industry, you are bound to come up with a few great ideas). Tactically, to improve skills and to ensure that franchisees are making sales calls, we focus resources and measure the results for the BrightStart and boost programs.

Beyond BrightStart and boost programs, we release a new "Idea Kit" every three to six months to focus a franchisee on a new customer type or referral source to incrementally improve her business. The Idea Kit includes a how-to guide showing who they will call on and what they will say, as well as a customized, targeted collateral piece to support the sales effort. As with targeted revenue opportunities within preexisting revenue verticals, I think it is critical for the senior leadership team, the Franchise Advisory Council, and the board of advisors to spend time considering what new revenue verticals could be developed by servicing new customer types with similar services or offering new services to existing customers. We expanded to provide care for children in addition to providing care for disabled adults and seniors; this was a strategy to use our recruiting efforts to service a wider array of clients (and after we personally had a need, when our twin boys were born premature at 28 weeks). Look to the aftermarket car care industry and their expansion into transmissions, oil changes, etc., for ways an industry can reinvent itself to extend its array of services to reach more customers.

Although we always need new customers, it is probably true that it is easier to sell more to existing customers than to find new ones. In our business, that means deepening relationships with those who refer to us, to gain a larger percentage of the business they refer out, or looking for incremental services our clients could use if we offered them, such as transportation to a doctor's appointment. For many types of franchise businesses, such as food and retail, it is important to prioritize strategies to increase the average dollars per ticket or per transaction.

Improve Gross Margins

Focusing on programs and initiatives to assist franchisees in improving their sales year over year are important and create a win-win for franchisees and the franchisor. For the franchisee's business and the system as a whole to be healthy long term, the business that franchisees add needs to have strong gross margins so that money falls to the bottom line; in other words, there needs to be a focus on adding "profitable new business." In addition to adding "good" business, initiatives need to be undertaken to assist franchisees in improving their gross margin.

In some industries, such as food, the cost of food must be continually looked at as well as processes to reduce spoilage and theft. Many industries also have the cost of labor in the cost-of-goods-sold area (like BrightStar does) that is part of the calculation of gross margin. To ensure adequate personnel and the retention of the best employees, wages have to be competitive, so cutting wages is likely not a viable option without negatively impacting customer retention. How, then, can we impact gross margin?

One way to impact gross margin is to cut costs in the cost-of-goods-sold category. If any of your costs other than wages are controllable, then plans should be developed to reduce these costs through better supplier negotiation and process efficiency. For BrightStar, we have worked to improve loss ratios through risk-management processes and training to drive down the cost of workers' compensation and professional and general liability insurance for our field staff employees. We also have worked on volume pricing for the costs related to readying an employee for work, such as background checks and drug screens, to positively impact gross margin.

Less obvious ways to assist franchisees in improving gross margin were two initiatives that went beyond supplier negotiations. First, we looked at opportunities to negotiate national or regional contracts on our franchisees' behalf in niche markets that have higher gross margins than most of the franchisees' locally generated revenue.

Second, we are investing in business intelligence tools—with a rules layer built on top—to alert franchisees when a client is below a target margin level so that they can take immediate action. We also can alert franchisees to non-billable overtime that negatively impacts their margin, because they may be unaware that their office personnel are scheduling cases in such a way as to require employees to be paid overtime that is not billable to the client (thus severely reducing margins).

BRIGHT IDEA:

Providing real-time information that a franchisee can use to improve the results of his business can have a positive impact on gross margin and overall results.

We also place an emphasis on helping franchisees understand how to sell the value of what they deliver and how their price is directly related to what they pay their caregivers. It is important to ensure we create the tools and training to prepare the franchisee to articulate her value proposition with customers and referral sources around pricing—customers of the franchisee need to understand that our pricing is slightly higher because our franchisees pay their healthcare employees more than market wages (usually by 2 to 10 percent) to attract and retain the best employees so the franchisee can deliver a higher quality and better service experience. We also have training tools for assisting franchisees in implementing price increases effectively with minimal or no loss in business.

Reduce Expenditures on Products and Services

We looked at the cost-of-goods-sold costs in the prior section. Still other expenditures can be reduced for the franchisee through active supplier management and helping franchisees identify opportunities to reduce expenses.

One of the largest expenses for many businesses is rent. It is prudent to take another look at the space requirements to see if they can be reduced. It is possible that you can negotiate with landlords to reduce rent. Sometimes the franchisor will need to step in and be a part of the discussion. At other times, the franchisor may be able to negotiate for multiple properties on behalf of various franchisees (particularly for retail space).

Beyond rent, anything that franchisees purchase at a local level should be evaluated for the opportunity to negotiate a national contract at a reduced price. Prioritize the evaluation of your suppliers based upon the amount spent on average by franchisees so you have a greater impact faster, and then continue through the list of suppliers. Once you have negotiated a supplier contract, don't consider negotiating to be done. If your number of franchisees or if the volume purchased by each franchisee increases, there is likely an opportunity to renegotiate.

I recommend that you include in your annual franchisee surveys a write-in opportunity to identify categories of purchases that franchisees feel would be less expensive if purchased for the entire national system. And to obtain deeper discounts, consider bundling multiple products and services with a particular supplier. For example, bundling payroll processing, 401(k), and insurance may result in better pricing than negotiating each separately.

Improve Efficiency

Now let's look at some initiatives that BrightStar has invested in to improve franchisee unit economics by assisting franchisees with improving productivity. We look for ways to allow franchisees to handle increased revenues with the same office labor, or minimal increases in labor, so that more money falls to the bottom line and the income percentage improves. Increasing revenue while holding office payroll costs level, or growing revenue faster than you grow office payroll costs, will improve the franchisee's revenues per dollar of payroll (using labor in the general and administrative [G&A] section and not labor in cost of goods sold). This is the ultimate metric for measuring efficiency.

BRIGHT IDEA:

One of the major breakthroughs we had was evaluating each function in a franchisee's business and matching the skills and experience required to accomplish the task.

We identified that we could retrofit the model in most states so that franchisees could have lower-wage personnel perform some functions full-time and have a higher-cost employee only part-time (rather than full-time) in the beginning. In any franchised business, the franchisee must constantly keep an eye on his employment decisions. These changes enabled the franchisee to make decisions that could result in improved employee retention for his business because the employees were better matched in skills and experience for the jobs they were hired for. These changes also allowed a reduction in franchisee personnel costs by approximately $25,000 per year.

We also identified opportunities to upgrade our technology so that it works for a franchisee's employees, allowing a more user-friendly experience. You hear my repeated emphasis on seeing technology as a game-changer and one of the best areas for you to invest in. Although there are many positives related to technology investments—such as the scalability, ROI, and competitive advantage benefits—there are also a couple of negatives. One is the amount of time it takes to complete large technology projects. Our technology upgrade, for instance, took nearly two years. Another negative is that you never make a *final* technology investment. As soon as you complete one project, you will easily be able to identify new ways to leverage technology for continued improvements.

We achieved a large efficiency breakthrough for our franchisees and for ourselves by implementing the support center (which you'll recall reading about in chapter 9). This center made it possible for franchisees and their office teams to receive a response to their requests, questions, or reported problems within four business hours. Rather than contacting their franchisee for process or technology questions and assistance, staff of our franchisees called corporate. All calls or online requests to the support center are logged into a system automatically, and reports are reviewed monthly to identify themes so that training can be adapted to address key knowledge gaps and/or so a franchisee can be alerted about possible competency issues with his staff.

It is great when we are able to identify ways to be of better service to franchisees and to keep them productive. It further helps us proactively identify improvements that we can make in the model, in our training, and in our online resources. We have also compiled frequently asked questions resources and a Wikipedia resource based on support center requests and franchisee-to-franchisee mentoring.

One of the biggest obstacles to continuous improvement within a franchise system to be mindful of is the rate of change introduced to the system. Corporate has much more bandwidth to identify system improvements than busy franchisees have to put these improvements into practice. It has taken us years to realize that bundling system changes into quarterly releases greatly increases the efficiency of adopting improvements. There is also the challenge of how to bring the early franchisees up to the same standards as those of the recently added franchisees as you grow. We discussed in chapter 9 the importance of continually training the franchisees and their core teams to current standards when I introduced the idea of investing in an online learning management system (LMS).

In addition to the LMS resources, we also began offering an annual Branch Leadership Conference (BLC) in our fourth year. We have held a franchisee conference annually since our second year to share best practices and communicate new processes to our franchisees. We realized, however, that the information was not consistently being communicated back to our franchisees' teams. We also understood that our franchisees were receiving continual education and professional development at their conference, but the franchisees' branch team was not receiving the same resources. The BLC provides a way for each franchisee's team to be developed and to ensure that brand standards are taught and then taken back to the businesses for brand consistency.

Closing Thoughts

The initiatives discussed in this section can and should begin from the first day you have a franchisee. As your franchisees mature, make a note to yourself that you will need new tricks to continue helping them take their businesses to the next level. Franchisees in their third or fourth year begin to benefit less from field support visits and need a new, non-traditional level of support. We learned from other franchisors how they use performance groups to bring together similar franchisees for summits to discuss the actions, hiring, and investments needed to reach the next level. We have just begun this process, and doing so has been our new breakthrough for helping those franchisees who were starting to slow their growth trajectory to create a new chapter for their business, reinvigorating them to get to the next level.

. . .

The next section stresses what is needed to differentiate your model in the eyes of your customers and what you must do to have your finger on the pulse of what customers think about the brand. You will learn how to leverage all that you've read throughout *Grow Smart, Risk Less* to consider the future possibilities of international expansion and/or the launch of additional franchise brands.

SECTION 5

ACHIEVING GROWTH AND SCALE

CHAPTER 12

Your Brand, Your Customers

A thorough discussion on building a sustainable franchise system would not be complete without a review of the ultimate responsibility of the franchisor: protecting the brand. From the beginning, the franchisor has to ensure that trademarks are secured and that collateral materials and the online presence positively represent the brand. What more should the franchisor be focused on as the brand relates to the end customer? Let's look at the key areas related to the brand: brand positioning, customer feedback, and cause marketing.

Brand Positioning

The franchisor needs to understand the brand's position in the market and leverage that in printed and online messaging. Are you the low-cost, high-quality, or high-service brand? The messages need to be consistent and your franchisees thoroughly trained on them, so that they understand your brand. At a recent International Franchise Association (IFA) conference I heard Frances Frei, a Harvard Business School professor, talk about achieving breakthrough service. She ventured that to be great at one thing (service or quality) you had to intentionally be bad at something else (price), and if you are not intentionally bad at one thing you will be mediocre at everything. Franchisees struggle with how to compete on price when others in their market are cheaper. As the leader of BrightStar, I have taken a stand and am leading our franchisees to focus on the areas in which we can drive quality and value so that customers focus more on those things and less on the price.

The franchisor constantly needs to innovate the offering to the customer. The franchisees and Franchise Advisory Council may make suggestions or pilot ideas, but it is the responsibility of the franchisor to implement, package, and train franchisees on new ideas and new offerings. The brand must be kept fresh and relevant in the eyes of the customer. This takes constant attention and investment. From inception, we have invested approximately 20 percent of our profits on market innovation (to fund the national ad fund in advance of receiving national ad fund contributions from franchisees) and service breakthroughs, and 20 to 50 percent on technology. The technology investment will lessen in future years, but the investment in innovation, or R&D, can't, if we are to continue to be the market leader in the eyes of our current and future customers. Our competitors will not sit still, so we have to constantly strive, invest, and think about ways to be better.

The franchisor must establish a differentiation in the marketplace for her goods or services and train, train, train the franchisees on how to market, advertise, and talk about their differentiation. Success in acquiring market share will depend on being the best in one area of differentiation—price, selection, time, quality, or service. When franchisees embrace and commit to the higher purpose of the brand, franchisees will be motivated to build the brand. This means that franchisors must spend the time to educate franchisees on the DNA, the soul, and the positioning of the brand *up front* in the recruitment process and continue to do so during training. If franchisees aren't clear on what the brand is and what it stands for, then they will spend more time reacting to competition (i.e., price) than building a brand that means to the community what you originally intended.

If you have appropriately engaged your franchisees in understanding the higher purpose of your brand and have made the right investments to create true differentiators, then competition will be irrelevant. In *Good to Great*, Jim Collins admitted that one of his biggest surprises was that all of his Level 5 leaders seldom, if ever, mentioned their competition. They almost always discussed how they wanted their companies to be perceived and designed marketing and advertising systems and strategies to bring that about. Put another way, they were never defined by their competition. That said, your franchisees will want to understand their competitors in the industry so they can verify that your brand is superior and follow you. Remember, franchisees do not follow blindly.

It will be beneficial for your franchisees if you assess the industry and equip them with information about how you are different from the perceived competitors, so they know how to sell against them at the local level. Keep in mind that many of your competitors will be doing the very same thing with respect to their brand. Healthy competitors and competition are good for everyone—it means that there is a demand for your products or services.

Customer Feedback

It is common to solicit feedback from your brand's direct customers because they have already engaged your brand's goods or services. It is necessary, though, to understand how all potential customers view your brand in the marketplace: If you don't assess how prospective customers perceive your business, you won't understand why your franchisee lost the opportunity to convert them to actual customers. As more customers share their opinion about brands online and seek advice from their online friends as to what brands to do business with, companies—particularly franchisors on behalf of the brand—must invest in understanding, and potentially improving, the perception of and the actual customer experience with their brand.

Before They Are Customers

Equally important as input from BrightStar's current customers is how individuals experience our brand before they become customers. Toward that end, we determined that an investment in a "mystery shopping process" could create a big breakthrough in helping franchisees improve their phone reception and client intake process. Every incremental improvement in how a potential client feels about our brand will increase the reputation of the franchisee at the local level and has the potential to increase revenues.

I would encourage all franchisors to think about building a mystery shopping program (in which a third-party company is hired to visit or call the franchisee's location to see what the experience is like, identify areas that can be improved, and report back to the franchisee and franchisor on the results) to help gather information about the experience of being in the shoes of the customer and to see how the customer perceives the brand. If you structure the program to focus on improving results through feedback, coaching, and retraining, such a program will hugely benefit franchisees. Do not use this type of program as a disciplinary program, because franchisees will not see this investment as being in their best interest. That said, if you see a pattern of poor performance in complying with brand standards after repeated mystery shops and attempts to improve compliance, you may need to proceed to stronger action.

Once They Are Customers

In addition to knowing what potential customers think about us, we find it critical to provide an outlet for our franchisees' existing customers through which they can let us know how we are doing. We send surveys to them through a third party to learn what we are doing well and what needs to be improved at the local level. Ultimately, we benchmark our franchisees on their customers' likelihood to recommend us to their friends and families (a measurement referred to as "net promoter score"). For locations that have lower than average net promoter scores, they are able to review the answers to the other questions on the customer survey to see what the particular areas of customer dissatisfaction are to make improvements in customer service, quality, or whatever areas are identified on the survey as not meeting customer expectations, to improve the franchisees' overall net promoter scores. We know that there is a high correlation between a franchisees' long-term revenue results to the net promoter scores, and we make the review of this information a priority for our franchisees and for our field support team.

If the idea of a net promoter score is new to you, make yourself a note to search for "Harvard Business Review Net Promoter Score" online (www.hbr.org). This measurement has revolutionized the ability to build processes to drive customer loyalty—once you recognize that customers who are merely satisfied are not necessarily loyal, you will begin to understand the need for a new measuring stick. The net promoter score is our new measuring stick to ensure that we are retaining our customers and using their experiences to attract new customers through their word-of-mouth promotion of our brand.

Selecting a vendor to monitor what your customers are saying about you is critical, and you may need more than one vendor to do this effectively. You need to understand who your customer is, especially if each transaction has multiple customers (a decision maker and a service recipient), and how each customer likes to be communicated with. At BrightStar we understand that most home care decisions are initiated and overseen by an adult child and that the senior parent is the service recipient. We also have learned that mail is the most effective communication tool with our seniors—with a response rate above 30 percent—and phone or e-mail is the most effective communication tool with the adult children. We subscribe to all three methods and have found them to be complementary.

More intensive surveys of customers can assist you in understanding where the customer expects improvement at the overall level, and these have been a critical component of our investments in driving more value and quality of care to our end customers. More limited surveys simply ask the key net promoter score question, "How likely are you to recommend us to friends and/or family?" This type of survey is more common, less costly to implement, and simple to adopt. The short survey containing only one question will enable you to provide a fast response to the customer: for promoters, to reward them for a referral, and for detractors, to respond to their complaint in a timely and proactive manner. A more thorough survey that asks this question but also asks about all the areas where your franchisee or their staff interact with the customer provides the expanded level of information needed to improve processes to actually improve customer loyalty overall.

Cause Marketing

In thinking about the brand from a broader perspective, factor in opportunities for cause marketing as you grow. Cause marketing provides an avenue to give back to a charity related to your business or the base of your employees in some way. Cause marketing also provides a method to highlight your brand as one that cares about the community and the greater good. Customers want to buy from companies with a conscience, that are socially responsible, and I believe the franchisor, through commitments of time and/or money (or both), can assist franchisees with participating in such events.

BrightStar Care aligned with the Alzheimer's Association initially because we understood that many of our end customers in our LifeCare segment have some form of dementia. In support of our KidCare segment, we added a charity focused on autism to show our commitment to a cause that impacts children. More important, we are a hugely community-oriented business, and our franchisees are passionate about promoting, raising money for, and giving time to charities. This provides a mechanism for our brand, our corporate personnel, and our franchisees to give back to the communities in which they operate.

As you consider a charity to support, nationally as well as locally, through involvement by your franchisees, I recommend that you choose a cause that all of your franchisees' customers will want to support unconditionally, like researching cures for multiple sclerosis or breast cancer. It's easy to alienate potential customers by aligning your brand with any cause that not everyone will want to support.

Closing Thoughts

Your system's success is ultimately based on the growth in the number of end customers. The franchisor needs to lay the ground rules and training for how to get customers, how to keep customers, and how to communicate with customers. It is too important to the mutual success of the franchisees and the franchisor to leave this to chance.

. . .

You have learned how to build a strong foundation for launching a franchise system. There may come a time when you are ready to expand further—either internationally or into additional franchise brands. Some franchise brands never expand beyond their initial country, and most franchisors only have one franchise brand. The choice will be yours. In the next chapter, we will explore the considerations for broadening your horizons.

CHAPTER 13

Building on a Strong Foundation

We have walked through the blueprints of expanding your business through franchising. At some point in the journey, you may begin to consider two additional methods of growth: expanding internationally or launching new, complementary brands. Let's look at some of the major considerations to determine when the time is right and how to prepare.

International Expansion

Many franchisors expand internationally too soon. Franchisors should first have a solid base of domestic franchisees, with a corresponding solid base of royalties, so that the franchisor is profitable and beyond the point of royalty self-sufficiency. When a franchisor expands internationally, it is critical that he can invest adequately to do it well. A franchisor needs to be committed to success in the international market, not just to collecting up front large master franchise fees. A franchisor must invest in dedicated international support, preferably in support personnel who have experience in the international markets that will be opened.

The U.S. Commercial Service has resources to help you determine whether international expansion is a viable option for your system—specifically by helping you to find out whether the goods and services you sell are desired in the countries you are targeting for expansion—on a country-by-country basis. You can research competitors to see if any of them have expanded internationally and how many locations they have opened in a given foreign country. This will help you determine if there is a market for international expansion and where you want to go. Once you make the decision to pursue expansion and have an idea of where you want to expand first, franchise industry resources can assist you with how to actually expand.

The International Franchise Association (IFA) has resources available to assist you with assessing different countries in terms of the franchise laws, the ease of doing business, and the business or industry laws in those countries. International franchise lawyers attend the IFA's annual convention (and annual Legal Symposium), and they will assist you with preparing the appropriate documents to comply with the franchise laws of the countries that you are interested in. International consultants can also assist you with designing a sales process targeted at international candidates and with selling international franchises.

It is critical to decide whether you will sell direct and support the international franchisees, or select master franchisees at the province or country level who will support the sub-franchisees locally. The decision should be thought through carefully, because the options differ in the level of financial commitment that you need to make up front and over time, and in your ability to control the brand. If you choose to expand internationally through master franchising, the selection of your master franchisee will be critical to protecting your brand and realizing the market potential. Master franchising is more common for service and retail franchise brands. Direct franchising is more common for food brands. The support mechanisms discussed in the following sections assume that a master franchising method is chosen.

International Support

When you are contemplating international expansion, you need to invest in hiring someone whose primary responsibility will be international operations, commonly called a director of international operations. The director will serve as the day-to-day contact for your international master franchisees and will work closely with them to adapt the website, marketing materials, operations manuals, hiring processes, and technology to accommodate the unique differences between the foreign market and the original model used in the United States. Ideally, your master franchisee will be required to open and operate her own location for at least six months or more (depending on your type of business) before being allowed to sell franchises; she must learn the business model thoroughly before the time comes to support her franchisees. The director will provide the primary support in assisting the master franchisee in opening her pilot location. It is also recommended to try, where possible, to select companies—rather than individuals—as master franchisees to leverage their existing infrastructure and to have a "partner" that understands franchising and the responsibilities the master assumes in exchange for an opportunity to split the royalties with the franchisor.

Ideally, a franchisor can hire key personnel (e.g., the director position) who live in or near the country they will support: for example, someone based in Europe to support Europe and someone based in Asia to support Asia. It is common for an American franchisor to expand first into Canada, where the first director will reside to support the first master franchisee, so the resource for the master franchisee lives close by to provide incremental support through all of the biggest lessons that will be learned on the first international expansion. Your first director will normally support the first three to five masters and, therefore, may also support master franchisees in several countries.

We will have directors supporting between four and eight masters, and these individuals will have no responsibility for supporting domestic franchisees. Having a separate internationally oriented team is important for two reasons. First, you won't upset domestic franchisees by shifting their support to handle international pursuits, and second, the international franchisees benefit from having dedicated personnel who understand their markets. Our first international director is based in Canada and has experience supporting franchisees in our industry in Canada, Australia, and the United Kingdom. As we expand into Europe and Asia, we will hire healthcare experts there to support our master franchisees. If we had expanded internationally prior to late 2010, we would not have had the resources to invest in this high level of support, which we believe is indispensable in a successful international expansion strategy.

Secure Intellectual Property

As soon as you believe that you may expand internationally, it is important to secure the trademarks for the countries you will expand into. We secured our international trademarks back in 2005, even though we didn't sell our first international master contract until 2010. As you are evaluating the competition and seeing to it that you have solid trademarks for your initial franchise system launch, you can research where your national competitors have expanded globally and which countries use the products or services you sell.

Many of the countries we knew we would want to expand into, because our domestic competitors had already done so, are signatories of the Madrid Protocol, which enabled us to secure trademark protection in several countries at once. The Madrid Protocol is the primary international system for facilitating the registration of trademarks in multiple jurisdictions around the world. When you get to this stage, compile for your trademark attorney the list of countries you eventually want to expand into and see how many are covered under the Madrid Protocol and what their filing costs will be. Then see which countries are not covered under the Madrid Protocol and the costs to file in each of the individual countries. Once you have the information, you can determine the amount you want to invest to ensure that your trademarks are preserved and protected when you are ready to launch globally.

Brand Expansion

It may seem strange to be talking about expanding into a second brand when you are just now evaluating how to start or expand your first franchise brand. And although it will likely be years before you seriously undertake an expansion to a second brand, it is nevertheless worth considering as part of developing your franchise disclosure document (FDD). It took me until late 2009 before I was clear on what additional brands I would launch in the future. Most franchisors will franchise only one brand. You, too, may franchise just one brand, but I encourage you to at least consider the possibility of brand expansion if you see an unmet need among your end customers that you could fill by launching another franchise system in the future.

You may be asking why you would consider launching more than one brand when you feel you will be plenty busy and challenged with launching one successfully. The biggest considerations are in how many franchise territories you can sell in your first brand and if expanding into new services will fill the unmet needs of your customers—or needs that your customers are buying through other companies. Let's explore each of these separately.

Timing of New Brands

For me, the consideration of how many territories I would sell under the BrightStar Care brand was a major driver for having more brands. I had commitments to 350 locations, and I knew that the United States would hold approximately 700 locations. Thus, within two to three years of solid growth and area development commitments, I would be sold out. I have great personnel in certain departments who are 80 to 100 percent focused on selecting or supporting brand-new franchisees, and if I no longer had territories to sell, I wouldn't have new franchisees to bring into the system. What would I do with my franchise sales team, my learning and development (training) team, my preopening concierge, and my BrightStart team? I had to find a way to keep my employees engaged, so launching new brands became of paramount importance to me.

The right time to launch my second brand was at the point at which certain departments began to have underutilized personnel because we were not adding as many new franchisees for them to support. I knew that expanding into new brands would be good for my personnel, and I also believed that offering new brands to my existing franchisees would be a good opportunity for them to diversify their asset portfolio and to create growth opportunities for their personnel. It had always bothered me as a franchisee of two different hotel franchisors that I was never given the opportunity to expand. I never knew a new site was planned until I saw a "Coming Soon" sign for a new hotel bearing one of my franchisor's brands.

In addition to creating growth opportunities for employees and franchisees, brand expansions can raise brand and market awareness of your existing services. Brands that can fulfill more of the needs of their customers help to ensure that those customers are not evaluating and using the services of other brands. Think about product brands such as SC Johnson or Johnson & Johnson. Would the parent company be a market leader if it had only one product? Or does it have such strong market brand awareness because its customers repeatedly encounter its various brands? It is difficult to find economies of scale in expensive advertising media such as radio and television when marketing for one brand alone, but it can be possible to reach more customers cost-effectively by advertising multiple complementary brands.

Market Need for New Brands

As you consider the creation of future brands, you must start with an understanding of what your customers are buying from others and/or what needs are not being met today. We worked with our customers to determine future brand opportunities by asking what other services they were buying for themselves in the healthcare area and what other services they purchased from others or needed in their homes. We then asked some of our franchisees the following three key questions: (1) Who is referring business to you today, and could you provide what they do? (2) Whom do you refer business to today, and could you provide what they do? (3) What types of competitors are you gaining customers from, and what types of competitors are you losing customers to? The insights from this kind of investigation will tell you what potential future brand opportunities there may be for you, for your employees, for your franchisees, and for your customers when you begin to have capacity in your organization to take on and adequately invest in these new brands.

As you determine what services your existing and potential customers need, you will want to evaluate whether these are services that can be easily provided under your existing franchise system. The consideration of whether additional products or services should be offered in the existing franchise system or offered in a new franchise brand is based upon two key factors: (1) whether you can offer the new services under the existing brand without confusion in the marketplace about your core competency, and (2) whether the new services fit within the operations and technology already in place without losing efficiency.

By way of example, when our customers needed transportation to medical appointments, we knew we had people to do it, and we knew it involved scheduling and matching employees with customers which are core to our existing business model. We therefore added transportation to our existing brand. However, when we realized that many of our customers were contracting with a handyman business, we determined that we did not want to dim our existing brand's reputation of high quality of care by creating the perception that we could care for our client's mom and plunge her toilet during the same site visit. If we decide that we want to be in the handyman business, it will need to be part of a different brand.

Additional Considerations

When you make the decision to expand internationally and/or to launch new brands, you have to communicate the news to your existing franchisees carefully. They have to clearly understand how they will be affected and why you are choosing this method of expansion. To gain your franchisees' support, there has to be a clear "what's in it for them" message, so that they grasp how they benefit from the launch of new brands.

When we began looking for our first international master, we proactively communicated to our system that once we sold our first two masters, we would use a significant portion of the cash flow benefit derived from the up-front master franchise fees to extend the billing cycle for their royalties (for those that joined BrightStar when the remittance cycle was 15 days to extend their remittance to that of the current standard of 28 days) by two weeks. We also made sure they knew about our investment in hiring an employee in Canada dedicated solely to supporting our international masters. Similarly, once we were ready to communicate our expansion into additional brands, I showed our entire strategy to all our franchisees at our annual convention. I described the benefits to the franchisees of their access to our corporate personnel that we would otherwise not be able to maintain if we didn't launch new brands, as well as the cross-sell benefit of these additional brands in terms of their existing customers.

In addition to the delicate nature of communicating further expansion to the existing franchisees, there is an important consideration in your selection of technology if you will expand internationally and/or expand into new brands. Although actual expansions may be years away, you need to consider the possibility at this stage to guarantee that you select the right technologies to scale and handle international differences, such as currencies.

BRIGHT IDEA:

Expansions into additional brands will also influence early decisions to build or buy software technologies to support your franchise system and to structure how you pay for technology.

If you will launch only one brand and you plan on a relatively modest number of units, then paying for the use of third-party technologies per franchisee may be optimal. However, if you believe now that you have the vision, passion, and organization to support growth into multiple brands, then you want to choose third-party technologies that sell enterprise licenses so that you can put unlimited numbers of users on the software. Based upon your future growth plans, you will also need to evaluate software programs according to the scale they are capable of handling.

Closing Thoughts

This entire book has focused on launching or expanding your initial franchise brand domestically. In this last chapter, however, I wanted you to think a little bit about the opportunities beyond the United States and beyond your first franchise brand. Although fewer than half of all franchisors expand internationally, there are considerations to evaluate early in terms of securing the trademarks in the foreign markets into which you may want to expand. Once you have success domestically and seriously begin to consider international franchising, you can access the various resources I have outlined to assist you in the discovery process, the legal document preparation, and the selling of franchises internationally. As you contemplate the services that your customers need but you do not yet provide, you may also consider the possibility of launching additional franchise brands. Most franchisors have one single franchise brand, but I encourage you to at least consider the employee, franchisee, and customer benefits of expanding and how to identify opportunities for expanding services within your brand or as a separate brand. In either expansion, international or brand, you will want to carefully consider how you will communicate this to your franchisees, so that they know about it first and understand how it will affect them.

Acknowledgments

Thank you to my husband, J.D., and my boys, Mike and Luc, for loving and supporting me while I spent the time writing this book. J.D., you were an integral part of our journey and have always been supportive of what I wanted to build.

Thank you to my friends and colleagues in the franchising industry for sharing their best practices, support, and friendship. A special thank you to those who reviewed the book prior to its publication: You provided amazing insight from multiple vantage points as leaders wearing legal, franchise sales, lending, investing, and public relations hats.

Thank you to my amazing franchisees and my dedicated, brilliant team for helping to build a franchise brand that has allowed me to help hundreds of new franchisors build great franchise systems and give their franchisees enthusiastic and tireless support. And thank you to my advisors and suppliers for working with me to continuously improve our system.

Thank you to the reader for the investment and commitment of your time to learning about how to leverage franchising to grow your business. I believe that you have already done the hardest work in creating a solid business from scratch. You should be commended for investigating ways to grow your business.

If you are ready to follow the step-by-step plan to franchise your business, you can achieve the same success that I have—or more. You must be committed to make the necessary investments in a scalable technology strategy and in building and empowering a great team. You must build a culture that is focused on franchisee unit economics and franchisee satisfaction. And, finally, you need to continuously improve, monitor the competition, and evaluate external trends to know how you are doing and to build the plan to be the best in your industry. As the leader, you own the responsibility for setting the vision, building the organization, and establishing the culture. Don't forget to enjoy the journey!

The Franchise Disclosure Document

The franchise disclosure document (FDD) contains 23 items that are required by the Federal Trade Commission for every franchisor.

The International Franchise Association provides a helpful overview of the 23 items on its website at: http://franchise.org/aboutfranchising.aspx. The 23 items are also described here.

Item 1: The franchisor and any parents, predecessors, and affiliates. This section provides a description of the company and its history.

Item 2: Business experience. This section provides biographical and professional information about the franchisor and its officers, directors, and executives.

Item 3: Litigation. This section provides relevant current and past criminal and civil litigation for the franchisor and its management.

Item 4: Bankruptcy. This section provides information about the franchisor and any management who have gone through a bankruptcy.

Item 5: Initial fees. This section provides information about the initial fees and the range and factors that determine the amount of the fees.

Item 6: Other fees. This section provides a description of all other recurring fees or payments that must be made.

Item 7: Estimated initial investment. This section is presented in table format and includes all the expenditures required by the franchisee to establish the franchise.

Item 8: Restriction on sources of products and services. This section includes the restrictions that the franchisor has established regarding the sources of products or services.

Item 9: Franchisee's obligations. This section provides a reference table that indicates where in the franchise agreement franchisees can find the obligations they have agreed to.

Item 10: Financing. This section describes the terms and conditions of any financing arrangements offered by the franchisor.

Item 11: Franchisor's assistance, advertising, computer systems, and training. This section describes the services that the franchisor will provide to the franchisee.

Item 12: Territory. This section provides the description of any protected territory and whether territories will be modified.

Item 13: Trademarks. This section provides information about the franchisor's trademarks and service and trade names.

Item 14: Patents, copyrights, and proprietary information. This section gives information about how the patents and copyrights can be used by the franchisee.

Item 15: Obligation to participate in the actual operation of the franchise business. This section describes the obligation of, and the extent of, the franchisee to participate in the actual operation of the business.

Item 16: Restrictions on what the franchisee may sell. This section deals with any restrictions on the goods and services that the franchisee may offer its customers.

Item 17: Renewal, termination, transfer, and dispute resolution. This section tells you when and whether your franchise can be renewed or terminated and what your rights and restrictions are when you have disagreements with your franchisor.

Item 18: Public figures. If the franchisor uses public figures (celebrities or public persons), the amount the person is paid is revealed in this section.

Item 19: Financial performance representations. This section provides the information disclosed on unit financial performance. All franchisors are allowed to include this information but doing so is not required.

Item 20: Outlets and franchisee information. This section provides locations and contact information of existing franchisees, as well as details on transfers and unit closures.

Item 21: Financial statements. Audited financial statements for the past three years are included in this section, as well as details on transfers and unit closures.

Item 22: Contracts. This section provides all of the agreements that the franchisee will be required to sign.

Item 23: Receipts. This section includes the receipt that prospective franchisees are required to sign acknowledging that they received the FDD.

Recommended Resources

Books

Charan, Ram. *Boards That Deliver* (Jossey-Bass, 2005).

Collins, Jim. *Good to Great* (HarperCollins, 2001).

Kiyosaki, Robert, and Sharon L. Lechter. *Rich Dad, Poor Dad* (Warner Books, 2001).

Rath, Tom. *Strengthsfinder 2.0* (Gallup Press, 2007).

Websites

www.growsmartriskless.com [code word: GROWSMART]

www.hbr.org Harvard Business Review Net Promoter Score

www.klososky.com (Scott Klososky)

Associations, Programs, and Events

Athena Power Link

Emerging Franchisor Conference

Franchise Update Media Group Leadership & Development Conference

Annual Franchise Development Report

Franchise CEO Summit

International Franchise Association (IFA)

International Franchise Association's Annual Convention

International Franchise Association's Certified Franchise Executive (CFE) Program

International Franchise Association's Executive Leadership Conference (ELC)

International Franchise Association's FranGuard Program

FranPAC (a political action committee)

FranShip program

Public Affairs Conference

Women Presidents' Organization

Franchisor Suppliers, Consultants, Etc.

Brand One/Kurt Landwehr (consultant)

Entrepreneur's Franchise 500 issue

FRANdata (supplier)

FRANdata's Annual Compensation Study

FRANdata's Business Credit Report

SBA Franchise Registry

FranSurvey (supplier)

Franchise America Finance (supplier)

Franchise Business Review (supplier)

Franchise Performance Group/Joe Mathews (consultant)

FranChoice (broker)

FranNet (broker)

MatchPoint (broker)

Process Peak (technology)

Proven Match (supplier)

Sandler (consultant)

SharePoint (technology)

The Entrepreneur Source (broker)

The U.S. Commercial Service

Franchisee Suppliers

See www.growsmartriskless.com for preferred partner list.

Index

F

internal team. *See entries beginning
with* "staff"
international expansion, 97, 238–39,
267–68, 269–70, 276
International Franchise Association
(IFA), v, 31–33, 34, 134, 234, 268
International Franchise Association
Annual Convention, 31, 32, 36, 42,
76, 268
international operations director, 97,
269–70
international support, 269–70
Internet portals, 153–54, 156,
171–74
investment range, 135–36, 172
investors vs. owner-operators, 168,
172
IPO (initial public offering), 203

J

Johnson, Jeff, 232
Join-the-Team Day (JTTD), 146–48

K

key metrics
BrightStar year-by-year, 86, 88,
94, 100, 105
franchise sales, 152–60
franchisors, 199–202
performance, 12
See also EBITDA; revenue per
dollar of payroll
Kiyosaki, Robert, 115
Klososky, Scott, 122

L

Landwehr, Kurt, 35, 136–37
launching a franchising system, vi–vii,
5–6, 22, 30–31, 36–38

lawyers
and FDD, 43–44, 127–28
and franchisee's validation process, 144, 145–46
franchising background of, 22,
33, 42–43
and international expansion, 268
on loaning money to franchisees,
194
for offering franchises without
initial fees, 179–80
of prospects, 146
on referral payments, 179
and sales process, 133
for trademark search, 23
leads
advertising, 171, 174–75
broker leads, 150–51, 155,
158–59, 160, 169, 175–78
franchise website, 170
Internet portals, 153–54, 156,
171–74
market awareness, 171
overview, 134–35, 169, 175
referrals, 178–79
suspects, 134, 135, 141, 153–59,
165–66, 172
See also prospects
lead generation, 153–57, 172
Leadership and Development Conference (Franchise Update Media
Group), 33–34
learning and development manager,
97
learning management system (LMS),
211, 212, 220, 241–42, 255
legal foundation
legal structure, 25
patenting and licensing technology, 24, 80, 90
trademarks, 9, 23–24, 270–71
See also lawyers
LMS (learning management system),
211, 212, 220, 241–42, 255

M

N

O